The White Women's Protection Ordinance
SEXUAL ANXIETY AND POLITICS IN PAPUA

The White Women's Protection Ordinance

SEXUAL ANXIETY AND POLITICS IN PAPUA

by

AMIRAH INGLIS

SUSSEX UNIVERSITY PRESS

1975

Published for
Sussex University Press
by
Chatto & Windus Ltd
40 William IV Street
London WC2N 4DF

*

Clarke, Irwin & Co Ltd
Toronto

———————

To

MANKA and ITZHAK GUST

My Parents

———————

First published in 1974 by Australian
National University Press, Canberra,
under the title *Not A White Woman Safe:
Sexual Anxiety and Politics in Port Moresby*
1920–1934

ISBN: 0 85621 049 8

© Amirah Inglis 1974

Printed and bound in Great Britain by
REDWOOD BURN LIMITED
Trowbridge & Esher

Preface

The Black Peril

Before Chief Judge Wanliss C.M.G.
The King v. Weira

Weira was charged with being in a dwelling house with intent to indecently offend a European female.

Headlines and beginning of story from *Rabaul Times*,
23 December 1927.

There are two ... aspects of social life in the Western Pacific that must be touched on—the 'Black Peril' and the 'Eternal Triangle'. It may be said that the Black Peril in Papua is not serious. Twenty years ago it scarcely existed. Civilisation, however, generally brings some trouble of this kind in its train.

Beatrice Grimshaw, *Isles of Adventure*, p. 28.

This book is about the passage by His Excellency Sir Hubert Murray of Papua of the White Women's Protection Ordinance of 1926. It was a piece of legislation discriminatory in its provisions, harsh in its penalties and startlingly out of character with Murray's 'native policy'.[1] No appraisal of Murray's rule and its effect on Papuans, no history of colonial Papua, can be complete without an explanation of it.

The White Women's Protection Ordinance was the most significant expression of one aspect of the relations between black and white in the colony, the fear of sexual attack by black men on white women and girls: the 'Black Peril'. The extent of this fear is perhaps hard to believe today, but any reading of the papers of the day will uncover it.

The Ordinance was extremely harsh and discriminatory by the standards of the time. No such legislation existed in any Australian state—where only in New South Wales and Victoria was death the penalty for rape—nor did it exist in any other colonial country whose legislation I have been able to read. It was not foisted upon the colonial government by the metropolitan power. The Lieutenant Governor of Papua was circumscribed by the provisions in the Papua Act of 1905 that all Papuan legislation was subject to the consent

v

of the Australian Government, and that the Papuan administration was bound by legislation initiated in Australia; but the White Women's Protection Ordinance originated in Papua. Murray was responsible for it.

In 1925 Hubert Murray published his second book, *Papua of Today*, and reviewed the achievements of seventeen years of his administration. It was an achievement, he declared (p. 9), that attacks on white women were rare and that there had never been one 'which remotely suggested an intention to commit rape'. Yet in August of the same year the white residents of Port Moresby petitioned Murray to protect their wives against sexual attacks by natives and demanded drastic action to deal with such offences. Murray ridiculed their fears and refused their demands. Not six months later, in January 1926, he had introduced an Ordinance to amend the Queensland criminal code (which operated in Papua) by providing the death penalty for any person convicted of the crime of rape or *attempted* rape upon a *European* woman or girl. How did he come to do it?

Why did Murray change his mind and change it so drastically between August and January? The question, so important to an understanding of Murray and of Papua's colonial history is not only unanswered in Francis West's biography of Hubert Murray, it has not even been asked. If the passage of the Ordinance is mentioned at all by historians of Papua, the measure is attributed to the white women who provoked attacks upon themselves by lax or inappropriate behaviour towards their servants and then bullied their husbands into forcing the Government to pass legislation to punish and deter those hapless victims of their own folly. Lewis Lett in his biography of Murray, J. T. Bensted (a former Director of Public Works in Papua) in his articles critically reviewing Lett's book, and Hubert Murray himself in many writings all offer this explanation.

Another belief is that the arrival of white women in Papua led to the worsening of relations between black and white. This can be used to explain sexual attacks—Margriet Roe gives an example from the Christian missions in her *History of South East Papua to 1930*; in this region, she says, easy social relations were almost impossible once the mission wives were established. But she gives no evidence for this. Writers on some other colonial societies agree in blaming white women for the hardening racial attitudes which, upon their arrival, crystallised into hard divisions what had formerly been more easy relationships, in particular between white men and black women. Caroline Ralston,[2] writing of other Pacific colonies, quotes O. Mannoni, Philip Mason and Herbert Moller in support. Philip Mason gives only partial support. Discussing the relations of the British in India with the Indians, he discerns that social distance between them grew as the nineteenth century advanced partly—but only partly—'as more English women came to India'.[3]

This book questions any explanation of the White Women's Protection Ordinance that rests mainly on the behaviour of the white women of Port Moresby, whether on their harsh exclusiveness or on their lax familiarity. There was an influx of white women into Papua during the twenties, but those who use this fact to explain the passage of the Ordinance bring forward no evidence of the connection and base the explanation simply on an unquestioned conviction that women always behave in a certain—wrong—fashion. It was the men of Port Moresby, and not the women, who were in the main responsible for the agitation and for the Ordinance and though they may have been influenced by the women this influence has never been demonstrated or explained.

In order to understand the passage of the Ordinance we have to see it as standing—not alone but the pinnacle of a structure of caste legislation—upon the conviction held by the most cultivated, enlightened and humane white men of the time, as well as the least, that the Papuans they ruled over, taught or converted, were an inferior race to themselves, one aspect of whose inferiority was the possession of sexual urges which were stronger than their own and which they could less easily restrain. There were differences in attitude towards Papuans between the planters and commercial interests on one side and the government and missionaries on the other, differences which broke out in many conflicts over the provision of native labour and in the political demands of the white residents for majority representation on the Legislative Council and in disputes over the extent to which traditional ways should be disrupted by work and education. But there was an underlying unity of belief and Sir Hubert Murray shared it.

This book was originally a thesis presented for the degree of Master of Arts in the Australian National University and deposited there. In the published version I have not given the names of any children or women. Nor have I given the names of the Papuans convicted of sexual offences, except for the two major characters and here I have changed their Papuan names but retained, in the case of the man who was hanged, the mission name by which he is still remembered in Port Moresby.

Port Moresby
1973

Acknowledgments

This book was written partly in Port Moresby and partly in Canberra and there are many people in both places to whom I am indebted. To the staff of the archives offices in both cities and to the staff of the Advanced Studies reading room of the National Library, Canberra, I am particularly grateful. In Canberra, Dr Dorothy Shineberg of the History Department, School of General Studies, Australian National University, was my most stimulating adviser, who read all my drafts with sharp eyes and provided important and helpful advice. Hank Nelson and Nigel Oram of the History Department, University of Papua New Guinea, read and commented, gave me the benefit of their wide knowledge of the history of Papua and allowed me to read their own manuscripts. Canon Ian Stuart, rector of the Anglican church of St John's, Port Moresby, read and commented on Chapters 2 and 3 and most kindly provided not only answers to queries, but also the information and the draft from which the map of the town of Port Moresby in 1930 was drawn. Susan and Ilinome Tarua, Moi Avei, Ted and Rosalind Wolfers in Port Moresby all read my manuscript. Jan Gammage typed it and the cartographers of the University of Papua New Guinea geography department drew the maps. I thank them all.

To those people, in Papua and Australia, who were alive at the time of which I write I owe a particular debt of gratitude. The late H. W. Champion and his son Ivan answered my questions on a touchy topic in long and interesting letters; Dr Percy Chatterton, retired London Missionary Society teacher, parson and former Member of the House of Assembly, did likewise. Mrs Mary Pinney, daughter of Sir Hubert Murray, told me of her youthful memories of government house. Stephen Ame and other men of Beipa'a village and Varuko Morea of Porebada village told me about their life in Port Moresby before World War II and what they knew of the Ordinance. Without all these the town would never have come to life for me.

To Murray Groves who first suggested this topic to me, who read drafts and made the most searching and critical comments, and to my husband, Ken Inglis, who read it all critically and helpfully and encouraged me not to give up, go my last and very special thanks.

Contents

Illustrations

Maps

Plates

x

One 'You can never be quite the same as the white man'

IN 1901 the members of the first Parliament of the Commonwealth of Australia debated Edmund Barton's motion that Australia accept control of British New Guinea. They said little about the inhabitants of the colony that the newly formed Australian nation was adopting, and showed scant knowledge of the people whose masters they were about to become, or of the land whose name they were about to change from British New Guinea to Papua. They believed that they were adopting 'savages' who were in their babyhood 'as far as civilisation and development were concerned' but who could be improved and civilised by good government and a proper protection of their interests. Later debates showed that protection of Papuan land against white speculators and of Papuan bodies against alcohol were foremost in the minds of the parliamentarians.

The Australians who introduced and debated the Papua Bill in 1903 and finally passed it in 1905 emphasised the helplessness and childlike character of the Papuans rather than their savagery; those who administered the Act in Papua, and who were faced with the pacification of the country, believed that Papuans were both savage and childlike, emphasising both traits at different times. An example was the Resident Magistrate C. A. W. Monckton, who believed that 'Kipling's definition of a native as "half devil and half child" is a very true one'.[1]

In 1906 the Commonwealth Government appointed a Royal Commission to inquire into the government of Papua. Witnesses from government, mission and plantation gave evidence that Papuans exhibited such childish behaviour as lying, loafing, carelessness and fecklessness. Earlier and later observers of Papuans had also found childish qualities. When allowed liberties, they did not fail to take advantage, noticed the English geologist Octavius Stone when he visited Port Moresby in 1875.[2] And in 1930, the childlike traits of going

1

over the odds and breaking promises were evident to the Government anthropologist, F. E. Williams, and described by him to Papuans in the monthly newspaper, *Papuan Villager*, which he published for the education of Papuans. White men, he wrote, unlike Papuans are allowed to drink and bet because they 'usually know when to stop'.[3] 'White people say', wrote 'Lagani-Namo', a European contributor, 'that Papuans will never do much good for themselves or anybody else until they learn how to keep their promises and this is true.'[4]

The childishness was partly seen as evolutionary. Papuans belonged to one of the 'child races' while the Europeans were adults in civilisation. Ideas of progress were abroad, theories of biological evolution[5] which easily translated into belief in the inferiority of the child races.

Missionaries, by definition of their calling, held pagan beliefs to be inferior to Christian and thus fell naturally into the role of new fathers with a duty to destroy customs which they found to be brutal or distasteful, and to replace old beliefs with new. Australian parliamentarians who had little knowledge and less experience of Papuans, and those missionaries, administrators, traders and planters whose knowledge and experience varied but were sometimes extensive, shared a belief in the inferiority of Papuans in civilisation, in morals and in social organisation. It was clear to all that their technical skills and material culture were inferior to those of Europeans and their way of life seemed to many bound to perpetuate that inferiority.

To some, village life seemed lazy. Many witnesses before the Royal Commission of 1906 observed that Papuans did not work, while even among those who did not grant the laziness of Papuans, like the Anglican missionary, A. K. Chignell,[6] and who perceived that they worked to a different rhythm from Europeans, like Anthony Musgrave[7] or Edith Turner, wife of the London Missionary Society principal of Lawes College,[8] it was possible to admit that 'a little more work, and a little harder work, might not be bad for these copper-coloured friends'.[9]

A vast amount of time and energy, it seemed to missionaries, were wasted on the organisation and production of

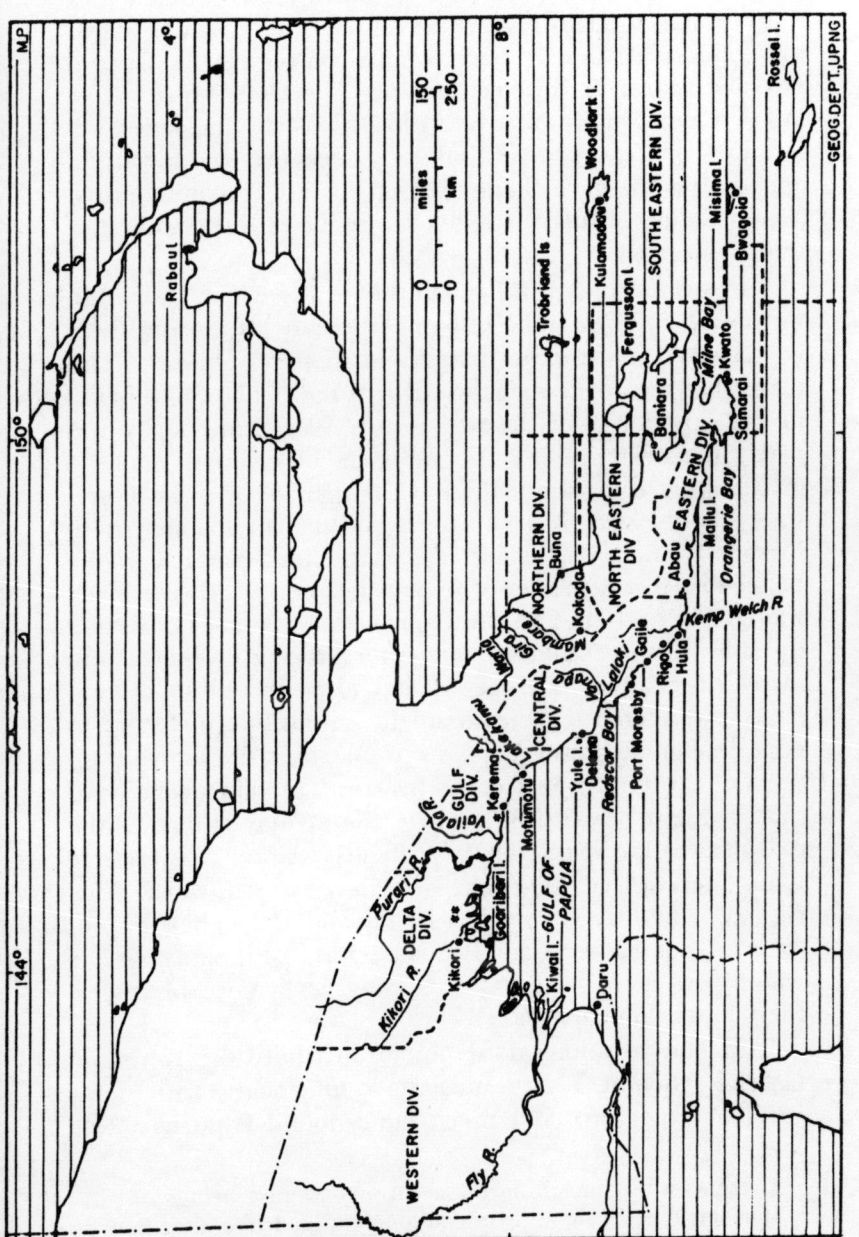

The Territory of Papua

feasts during which quantities of food were consumed in a wasteful and thoughtless manner. A relentless war was waged by London Missionary Society missionaries in the Central Division against traditional dancing. The Motu dance, wrote W. G. Lawes, was 'a carnival of licentiousness and sensuality . . . all work (except that absolutely necessary) was given up, and the people gave themselves up to lust and immorality. The meaning of the dance, the *raison d'etre* for its existence was fornication.'[10]

It was not only the Papuan way of life which seemed to Europeans inferior and likely to perpetuate inferiority; there was an even more important strand in the complex of attitudes that the white men brought to their subjects, a belief in the superiority of the white 'race'. This superiority was partly demonstrated by the very fact of colonial life: 'no matter what the reason, these white men seem to be bosses wherever they go' was how F. E. Williams explained it to literate Papuans.[11] Perhaps it was this fact that led to the belief in a sort of ladder of human races on which the black was on the bottom, and the Papuan came perhaps one rung up. The Royal Commissioners, after hearing evidence from many experienced Europeans and after travelling around Papua, wondered whether it might be possible in future to educate enough young Papuans to take over the junior positions of the Public Service, as Indians had. They concluded that it might be possible though 'the mental calibre of the two races is far apart'. F. E. Williams, writing twenty-three years later, agreed. When he described the Australian Aborigines to his Papuan readers he said lightly: 'They are not so good-looking as some Papuans; but then, some people who know them well, say that they have more brains, so their looks don't matter.'[12]

In one very important human attribute the Reverend Charles Abel of Kwato mission, a missionary with many years of experience and much fame, found Papuans rating low.

> It seems a terrible thing to say of any human beings . . . but it seems true of these people among whom I live, that they do not know what love is . . . I know of no animal, except perhaps

4

the duck, which is more careless in attending to its young than the average Papuan mother.[13]

Hubert Murray, whose attitudes were based not only on received beliefs but on knowledge, experience and a clear-headed, unsentimental and honest understanding of some of his own prejudices, thought and wrote a good deal about the inferiority of Papuans. After thirty years as Lieutenant-Governor he wrote: 'Europeans as a whole have an innate superiority over Papuans.'[14]

Belief in the superiority of the white race imbued alike those who wanted to protect Papuans from exploitation and those who wanted to exploit them; those who wanted to transform them into Europeans and those who believed that the customs and traditions of primitive societies should be interfered with as little as possible if they were to survive contact.[15]

Some aspects of a belief in white superiority cut across the paternal belief that Papuans were children in civilisation who could be taught, like all children, to grow up like their parents. For no matter how hard a member of an inferior race tried, his inferiority could never be overcome. The activities of missions and government in Papua in educating, protecting and guiding all implied a conviction that inferiorities in education, technical skills and morality might well be overcome, but took for granted that no amount of giving up dancing and other foolishness, no amount of embracing Christianity, no amount of going to work, or learning English could make the Papuan an equal.

The more the primitive Papuan came into contact with the civilising Europeans, the more he tried to model himself on them—and the more he succeeded—the less many of them liked him. Some even scorned his attempts to learn the new ways. By the mid-1920s the first of a long succession of stories about some stupidity perpetrated by half-educated Papuans began to appear in the press. For example, 'Tauwarra' wrote in the *Bulletin*, 11 November 1926, about a 'Hanuabada native electrician' who, having forgotten which of the two wires was live, got his offsider to touch one. The offsider fortunately lived. These stories were told by men who

5

thought Papuans should never have been educated at all; even those who did think it good to educate Papuans often had an ambivalent attitude towards the fruits of this education. The *Papuan Villager* was begun in 1929 as a serious government venture to educate Papuans in the ways of the white man and also in the ways of each other. After a year it had 179 Papuan subscribers and 208 European; after two years 230 of its 307 subscribers were Europeans.[16] Europeans were 'considerably attracted to it' wrote H. W. Champion and he noticed that the halting style of English used by the Papuan contributors 'makes us smile'.[17] F. E. Williams and Hubert Murray, both of whom were committed to improving the Papuans, felt, with many other Europeans, that Papuans acquired only the least noble, or the least important aspects of civilisation and were in danger of becoming a 'tenth-rate type of European'.[18]

With every new way learnt from the white man, the elusive goal of civilisation seemed to recede still further from Papuans. It was clearly civilised to cover the body since Europeans did it and so Papuan adults were forced to wear a loin cloth in towns where they came in contact with Europeans. But when Papuans emulated Europeans to the extent of wearing clothes all over, then wearing clothes for Papuans was not proper. So in 1922 Papuans were forbidden to wear too many. The Native Regulations of 1922 stated: 'Except as hereafter provided natives whether male or female are forbidden to wear clothes on the upper part of the body' and explained this as a health measure, and a protection for those 'foolish men and women' who wore dirty and wet clothes and made themselves sick. But Williams told his Papuan readers that wearing clothes was one of the white man's ways which they should not try to emulate. 'You can never be quite the same as the white man; and you will only look silly if you try to be. When we see a native in European clothes we usually laugh at him.'[19] It could be explained too as a matter of aesthetics. In 1934, on the fiftieth anniversary of the Proclamation of the Protectorate by Commodore Erskine, those Papuans who could read enough English to follow the *Papuan Villager*'s account learnt that:

The biggest chief of all, had an old shirt on. He also had some green leaves stuck in a hole through his left ear. The green leaves in his ear probably made him look better, like some green lettuce on a plate of sandwiches. But I'm sure the old shirt did not. Think of a plate of sandwiches covered with an old shirt. What would your *Sinabada* say?[20]

The regulation was understood by the Papuans who suffered under its provisions as 'the Government's way'. 'In those days government only wanted whites to cover the skin, not natives', recalls Stephen Ame, of Beipa'a, a Mekeo village in the Kairuku sub-district, who worked in Port Moresby before the war. Police tore the singlets off the backs of Papuans who, unaware of the law, had bought them in stores.[21]

Other white men's ways were disapproved of for Papuans. If white men gambled in their leisure hours and Papuans imitated them, then gambling for Papuans was not civilised and a regulation was passed in 1908 forbidding 'any native' to play cards for money or money's worth or to gamble in any other way. The penalty was a fine of £2 or imprisonment for a period not exceeding four months. When Papuans tried to emulate the white man's way of building his houses, this too was frowned upon. Murray and Williams both deplored the structures with iron roofs that were going up in Port Moresby villages. 'We like to see the Motu and Koita houses', wrote Williams. 'If you build one like a European copra shed it will not look very pretty.'[22] To become civilised obviously involved the very difficult process of choosing exactly which of the white man's ways to emulate; but whichever a Papuan chose did him little good.

The Papuans who came into contact with civilisation were not only disliked but were feared for aping Europeans. The villager in the bush lived a life completely different from that of the European who came to rule over him. In the village, hunting, farming and living by traditional rules, he was a threat to the physical safety of the European only in so far as he was warlike, armed and hostile. He might kill an intruder who wandered into his territory or he might become hostile for a particular reason against the bearers of the new dispensation, their police or their gaols. He might, as did the murderers of Weaver in 1906, kill a man for some reason which the white men found difficulty in comprehending. The white men were always in control; and this savage behaviour, though disliked and feared, was not resented. It was what one expected. But once the bush villager gave up some of the old ways and started to try and live like a European to the extent of becoming a Christian, abandoning traditional ways of settling disputes and traditional patterns of gift exchange and trade, wearing clothes—or trying to—paying taxes, working for wages, acquiring an education in English, then many of the white inhabitants resented him as a threat to their superior position. Now the Papuan began to have ideas of his own worth above those of his station of ignorant bush villager or servant which were his by right of his race, and the residents saw him as 'cheeky' or 'spoiled', a deterioration always the result of the 'influence of civilisation', and already remarked on as early as 1906, in evidence before the Royal Commission.

Alice Jeanetta Keelan, wife of an officer in the Papuan government service, who had worked in many parts of Papua from 1908 to 1924, found that during the latter years 'arrogance and conceit as well as a tendency to regard the white race with contempt, if not absolute disrespect, and thinly-veiled hostility' had come over the Papuans; and she found this change a direct result of 'legislation and education originally designed for their protection and uplift'.[23] F. E. Williams observed the resentment which Europeans showed to 'civilised natives' and explained it as the result of race prejudice. 'Wherever the "colour-line" is strongly defined', he said, 'as it undoubtedly is in all British dependencies' this resentment existed. It 'is widely-spread and . . . deep-seated, and as such it is a force to be reckoned with'.[24]

This 'deterioration' in Papuans was most noticeable in the towns. It was in the towns that Papuans had sufficient knowledge of Europeans' ways to imitate many of them; it was in the towns that the white residents most feared them. Hubert Murray had said that only the people of the Gulf Division had seemed to the government a likely threat to its power because they had very large villages and a tighter form of social organisation than had been encountered else-

8

where in Papua. But fear and resentment did not enter the voice of white men writing about Gulf men until they came to Port Moresby to work as servants. Then the 'grinning Gulf natives' were seen as a threat and legislation was passed to keep them out of town. A similar phenomenon was observed in the Union of South Africa in 1913 by the special commission appointed by the government to inquire into attacks on women. 'In the olden times', said the commissioners, 'crimes of sexual assault by natives upon white women were practically unknown . . . Little doubt can therefore be entertained that these are due to depravity engendered among natives by contacts with the evils of civilisation.'[25]

Papuans were seen to be particularly susceptible to the evils of town life. 'Birmingham or Manchester', wrote missionary Chignell, 'may be the making of the country lad, if he has any real grit in him, or it may be the sheer ruin of him if he is of the weaker sort. And these Papuans have no particular character or grit or moral strength; and three years on a plantation, or in a mining camp, or at Port Moresby is, more often than not, enough for their complete undoing.'[26]

The attitudes of Europeans towards the first pacified group of Papuans—those Motu and Koitapu people who felt the intensive influence of mission and government—are significant. Not only do they exemplify the phenomenon just described and also the caste nature of European behaviour, but they suggest that there were never harmonious and equal social relations between coloniser and native inhabitant, which it has been said came to an end as a result of the arrival of a large number of white women. No matter how much they tried to conform to European ways, no matter how soon they gave up fighting and other traditional behaviour, Papuans were never accepted as equal to Europeans, even by those who treated them kindly and with sympathy, and they were often despised precisely because they attempted to emulate white men.

When Captain John Moresby first saw the Western Motu people at Redscar Head in February 1873, he remarked on their charm, describing them as 'small, lithe copper-coloured people with clean well-cut features and a pleasing

9

expression of countenance'.[27] W. G. Lawes was more lyrical: 'The men are light in colour—a warm brown—and neither tall nor stout. They are muscular and well-developed, upright in their gait, and agile in their movements.' Their features conformed to European standards of beauty. 'You rarely see the receding forehead and protruding jaw so characteristic of some dark races. Their noses are fairly well-formed and their lips neither protruding nor thick',[28] wrote Lawes and he thought the women matched the men in grace and beauty. James Chalmers described the women at one of his services in the village of Hanuabada and said that their 'persons were quite exquisitely tattooed'.[29] European taste favoured light coloured, smooth skin and the people here pleased the missionaries more than the darker and more strongly featured people they had seen in the Gulf or Delta villages.

The Port Moresby Motu, though a powerful and belligerent people among the inhabitants of the coast, had not hindered either the European missionaries or the government from taking up residence in their midst. The London Missionary Society's white missionary and the Government's chief officer each had a house built within half a mile of the Village (as Hanuabada was called), and each on hills which looked down on the village cluster. The Motu exhibited other mild characteristics. In 1884, Chalmers reported, when a warrior died on a Sunday, 'in deference to the wishes of the missionaries, drums were not beaten . . . until midnight, when the full wail for the dead began, and continued till about ten p.m. of Monday.'[30] 'The Motu are certainly a quick and intelligent people, pleasant and easy-going in disposition' was Murray's verdict in 1912. But these very peaceful qualities and the marks of quick learning which might have endeared the Motu and Koita people to their rulers were deprecated and even despised. Murray, who described them as excellent boatmen and good domestic servants, added that they were useless as carriers and reluctant to join the constabulary, being loath to go far from home and being 'even more than other natives, averse to discipline and hard work'.[31] Both H. L. Griffin, Resident Magistrate of the Gulf Division, and C. A. W. Monckton, Resident Magistrate of the Northern Division, in their evidence before the 1906 Royal Commission sneered at the Motu for their 'weakness', and the Commissioners were convinced by this and other evidence that the natives of the Northern, North Eastern and Western Divisions represented the 'pick and flower of Papuan manhood, and were as superior as fighters, to the Motuan tribes, as are the Rajputs to the weak and effeminate natives of Bengal and Madras'. In the words of the Commissioners the Motu inhabitants of the Village were 'useless'. Even the Resident Magistrate of Central Division, in which the Motu and Koita villages found themselves, had not much to say for them, and agreed that they had been 'a far better race when they always had to be on the *qui vive*'. The Port Moresby natives, he said, had 'become a little more cheeky. Of course, the more they come into contact with the white man they become more cheeky.' But no one in 1906 suggested that these 'cheeky' Hanuabadans might have carnal designs on white women, only that they were insolent—'the most pampered lot of lying lazy loafers in New Guinea'[32]— disobedient, without moral fibre and that they would not get out of one's way on the streets of Port Moresby.

By 1925 the situation had changed. The white resident population had grown, Port Moresby had developed into a larger and more settled European town and now 'cheekiness' was seen by the residents expressed in those sexual advances which 'had chiefly occurred in Port Moresby and its environs, where coddling missions and armchair officials encouraged the flash Hanuabadan to flights of insolence not attempted by the natives of more enlightened districts situated at a distance from bureaucracy'.[33] Yet no Hanuabadan was involved, then or later, in any of those attacks on white women which came before the Central Court in the 1920s and 1930s.

Because relations between black and white deteriorated as Papuans became acculturated, some white residents assumed that the Hanuabadans, who lived closest to the European style, must therefore be responsible for sexual attacks.

The nature of the sexual relations between a dominant and a subject people depends on many things, including the sexual mores of each group, the caste relations between them, class, and such accidental factors as the availability of partners among the dominant people and how attractive the dominant people find their subjects. When the rulers are white and the subjects black, the deep-seated identification in European culture of blackness and evil emerges. This has been much discussed by writers on race relations and there are many examples from Papuan experience.[34]

In Papua (as elsewhere), many whites believed that people in primitive societies were more animal in sexual matters than people in sophisticated ones, that they were naturally gross-minded. The Papuan servant, wrote 'Molo-kihi', a correspondent to the *Bulletin*, though he appeared 'child-like and bland' was a normal human being with very strong sex instincts.[35]

Some white people found that Papuan sexual mores were different from their own, and this tended to confirm their assumptions about Papuan gross-mindedness. When Hubert Murray paid an official visit to Dopima village in the Gulf of Papua, he was made welcome, mats were put down, food prepared and, he noted in his diary, that 'they wanted to give us women, also to kill a dog for us'.[36] Murray believed that Papuans had commonly less sexual restraint than white men.[37]

The sexual freedom allowed to unmarried youth in some Papuan societies caused much concern among the missionaries, and the sexual proclivities of the inhabitants of the western Divisions, especially the Gulf and the Delta, seemed to missionaries peculiarly distasteful. Edith Turner, describing the women of the Purari delta in her pamphlet *Among Papuan Women*, quoted the Reverend J. H. Holmes: 'Their life is so pollute, so bestial, so unlike anything ever associated with women of any country that I can only describe it in the most casual way.' From her own observations, Mrs Turner feared that what Mrs Chalmers had written from Saguane in 1898 remained true in 1920. 'The immorality, from our standpoint, is fearful. The girls here take all the initiative. If they fancy a man or boy, they just go and fetch him or persuade him to go off into the bush with them.'[38] While it was female sexuality which Mrs Turner described, it was easy for her readers to believe that in such an atmosphere of

12

permissive sexuality, anything might happen and that boys and girls brought up thus would not be restrained adults.

Sexual relations between black and white in Papua were almost always between white men and black women, and so far from showing evidence of happy harmonious relations before the arrival of white women put an end to them, many of the liaisons are evidence of exactly the opposite, of contempt, of sexual and racial patronage. This becomes clear in any description of these sexual relations in fact or in fiction. There was, in the 1920s, a great taste for the literature of the South Seas among Australian readers. Two of the most popular writers were Beatrice Grimshaw and Jack McLaren, both of whom had experienced life in Pacific Islands. Beatrice Grimshaw, an Irish-born travel writer and novelist, settled in the hills outside Port Moresby, became a close friend, admirer and supporter of Hubert Murray, and lived and worked for many years in Port Moresby where she was widely read by the white residents. The two themes of her adventure romances are race pride and race purity. Her heroes never besmirch themselves by sexual relations with Papuan women and not simply because these relationships are always dishonourable and degradingly impermanent and broken as soon as the white man brings in a white wife.[39] Not even Simon, a white man raised by Papuans from infancy until he reached sixteen years, then educated in Sydney, Oxford and on Gallipoli, a man who had chosen to renounce Western civilisation for the simple island life, not even Simon will take an island wife. 'I respect my race . . . I will not throw back the course of evolution. I will have no son or daughter a hundred thousand years behind myself,' he explains to a visiting white friend. There were men, he admitted, who in his situation had taken brown wives, or 'half-castes' but not him. 'White Australian to the roots of my soul, I would not give my name nor the mothering and care of my children to a woman with one dark drop in her veins.'[40] In the novel he is not condemned to the celibacy which would have been his lot in life, for Beatrice Grimshaw provided White Savage Simon with a white girl who, like himself, had been stolen by natives as a baby and now, with her long gold hair, was the pride of the villagers.

The stories by Jack McLaren and other men who wrote novels about Papua are equally concerned with race purity, but are gamier, being about a rougher type of man, and make more allowances for the sexual needs of white men (and black women). Everyman's fantasy of smiling, willing and passionate island girls who may be had with ease, bring no responsibilities and are just as easily put away when necessary is not a picture of racial tolerance and equality. All the rights are on the side of the white man. Here is one account of such a situation. 'There was something wonderful about it all, this great swell of passion for him in a handsome girl he had seen for the first time that day,' mused the amazed and delighted white hero of Harold Mercer's *Amazon Island, A Romance of the Pacific*. Wonderful indeed, since the handsome girl had not only seen him for the first time that day, but had swum across a shark-infested sea to climb over the side of his boat and into his bunk.

Similarly we have the story of Subuna, a beautiful coastal Papuan girl who loved a white trader with a Papuan passion. But he had made it a strict rule 'that no native woman or girl entered his house . . . Many a good, decent man had ruined his prospects himself'.[41] Though McLaren will not allow his young trader to succumb to Subuna, rightly portraying such relationships as without honour, he provides much titillating in the refusal.

The male writers, whether they portray romances between white men and black women, or refuse to countenance them, show them to have been the relations of inferiors with superiors. Their heroes married, and therefore respected, *only* white women. At the same time, male writers built the notion of 'the White Woman', an object frail, respectable, passionless, calm, cool, clean and unable to stand either the hardships or the wild passions of the tropics. Beatrice Grimshaw's heroines are different: perhaps a projection of herself, they ride fearlessly through the bush to visit sorcerers. They behave like country women, or like those other women travellers Mary Hall (1914), Philippa Bridges (1924) and Evelyn Cheeseman (1935) who walked through Papua with guides and carriers collecting insects, or observations or material for novels. Beatrice Grimshaw's advice to white

14

women faced with the 'Black Peril' was to learn how to use firearms and to keep them in the house.[42] But Jack McLaren's women are very different. One of them says: 'This may be beautiful enough and all that, but it is uncivilised and crude. It is no place for a white woman, and I'm sure I shall not breathe freely again till we are back in Sydney.'[43] A McLaren hero, a thirty-year-old gold prospector, describes a long canoe trip as 'No trip for a white woman' and 'native truck' as 'no food for a white woman; it's bad enough for a man.'[44] This white woman—who always had to be protected—on whose behalf good white heroes eschewed native women and bad white villains disposed of them—is, like the passionate swimmer, a male invention and the source of much of the belief in the happy past of carefree sexual relations between black and white.

There was much intercourse between white men and black women, but the reality was very different from that presented by the romantic novelists, in that many men— unlike Grimshaw's heroes—did take Papuan women into their houses and their beds, and—unlike Mercer's—they rarely sat passively while the brown beauties swam to them. The white men who first came to Papua were missionaries— who were either married as a matter of church policy, or celibate—and traders; later came miners, planters, a few seamen and artisans and members of the government service. From the earliest days of white settlement, white men had had access to Papuan women and though public servants were prohibited from cohabiting with native women under pain of dismissal some did.

In 1908, Army Henry Jiear, Resident Magistrate of the Western Division, was asked to resign for cohabiting with a native woman.[45] In 1909 the Resident Magistrate of the Eastern Division, then on duty with the Anglo-German Boundary Commission, was charged by a sergeant of the Armed Native Constabulary with having ordered village constables and members of the Armed Native Constabulary to procure him native women. After eight sittings of the Executive Council the charges were found proven and the officer, of long and excellent service, was suspended and allowed to resign. As part of the evidence, one of the many

15

Papuan witnesses said that when she was told to go to the Resident Magistrate she demurred, saying, 'I do not want any more white man. White man been having me all the time'. She was paid, she said, ten sticks of tobacco for two visits and added, 'I liked long Mr . . .'.

In 1913, another Resident Magistrate, of the North Eastern Division, was relieved of his duties for cohabiting with native women. A member of the Anglo-German Boundary Commission against whom similar offences were alleged in 1910 denied them as patently false: 'Can it be conceived that any white man would do such a thing?', he wrote in his defence to the Government Secretary.[46] These cases came before the Executive Council because high government officials were alleged to be using their power and prestige to force women, or because complaints of rape or near rape had been made by Papuans. None was dismissed with ignominy, nor were the cases published. None of these men was charged with rape, though in the case of the Boundary Commission official it was alleged that one woman had had to be held down by villagers.

There were more permanent unions. Officially frowned on—and forbidden to government servants—concubinage was common enough to be regulated. W. E. J. Buchanan, a resident of Papua since 1897, thought the regulation which forbade a white man from taking a woman from the district without marrying her was 'very oppressive to a certain class of white man' and likely to lead to bigamy. A man should be allowed to take her, provided he gave a proper guarantee to restore her to her village, he told the Royal Commissioners in 1906.

Hubert Murray noted in his diary for 1909 from Aikora, a gold mining settlement in the Northern Division, that there had been a raid on the miners' camp during which 'the natives carried off two Waria women belonging to Stone and Erickson'. George Hunter, sandalwood getter and Government Agent at Rigo in 1888, twin brother of Robert, had a Papuan mistress who murdered him by jumping on his chest while he was drunk. She was imprisoned in Port Moresby for six years, until 'some of the European ladies of the town' succeeded in having her released.[47]

Some unions were legal marriages. There was no law in Papua equivalent to the Marriage Ordinance of the Mandated Territory which declared it unlawful for a registered clergyman or a district officer to marry 'a native with any person other than a native' without the written permission of a district officer. Hubert Murray had noted in his diary that one, Martin, was living with a Hula woman of 'very bounteous charms, very scanty rami [lap lap]', by whom he had had two children. He married her in 1916. Between 1892—when the recording of marriages began—and 1940, thirty-seven marriages between Europeans and Papuans were recorded, not including marriages with mixed race people. All were between European men and Papuan women. Sixteen of the thirty-seven were traders, seven were sailors and five miners. None was a clerk or a government official. The men were much older than their Papuan wives who were mostly young girls: twenty-seven of the husbands were between thirty and forty-nine, and seven were fifty years or older; thirty-five of the wives were between thirteen and twenty-nine. The youngest bride registered was thirteen years old. In contrast, the European men who married European wives in Papua often married women several years older than themselves. R. E. Guise, grandfather of the first Papuan speaker of the House of Assembly, married his Irupara wife in the year before he died. Robert Hunter, twin of the murdered one, was legally married to a woman of Tatana village, according to H. W. Champion's recollection. She was a woman who spoke English well, wore European clothes and often took lunch or afternoon tea with Mrs Champion, which suggests that in the case of at least this white woman, approval was given to legal marriage. Married women have never been partial to concubinage.

Many of these marriages were impermanent. The carpenter who married his Tatana wife in 1902 applied for custody of his two children four years later, undertaking to send them to school. He was granted custody, a fact which Murray noted in his diary for 1906. Almost none of these names appears again in the marriage register. If children resulted from the marriages, they must have taken Papuan names and disappeared into the Papuan communities of their mothers.

Twenty-three of these thirty-seven marriages occurred between 1896 and 1903, and during those years they made up 7 per cent of all marriages registered. The remaining fourteen were scattered between 1908 and 1924. Between 1924 and 1940 no marriage was registered between a European and a Papuan, though there were a few marriages between mixed race girls and Europeans. If this appears to support the argument that the arrival of white women widened the gap between black and white, the appearance is misleading. The arrival of white women during the 1920s was a consequence of the growth of the towns of Moresby and Samarai and the more settled nature of life in Papua. The sort of men who had married Papuan girls between 1896 and 1924— traders, miners and seamen—became less numerous in Papua as gold became scarce and copper mining failed. The white men who came to Papua in the 1920s and 1930s came to take up occupations in which respectability was more valued. They married white women if they could get them.

Captain Barton, the Administrator whom Murray replaced in 1908, had thought concubinage a good thing for a government officer because he 'thereby learnt the language which more than counterbalanced any objection'.[48] But Barton was an Englishman and Murray an Australian who strongly disapproved of this view and brought it up in his evidence before the Royal Commission in order to discredit Barton. It was not common for government or missions in Murray's time to approve sexual relations between black women and white men both because these relations were usually irregular and because they produced half-caste children and endangered that racial purity which Australians valued so highly.

Bishop de Boismenu of the Roman Catholic Mission at Yule Island was one who deplored temporary unions. In 1920 he wrote a long letter to the Lieutenant-Governor, placing before His Excellency the facts of a 'growing problem' of half-caste children and deserted girls. The growing number of half-caste children was a problem because 'Australian principles have no solution other than racial ostra-

18

cism' for such children. Another strand of the problem was that the success which white men had with Papuan women was beginning to arouse in 'native boys gifted with logical minds, certain bold aspirations which might easily carry them on to mad enterprises likely to end one day in lynchings'. Finally, de Boismenu objected because the unions between white men and black women were 'deceptions on the part of the white party who avowedly regards them as temporary arrangements while the girl is almost always led to regard them as permanent and serious ones'. Half-Papuan girls, even more than any other, he felt, were exposed to this danger and more defenceless. He asked the Lieutenant-Governor to interfere, not in any belief that such unions could be successfully forbidden but so that they could be made 'costly and consequently rare'.[49] The Executive Council considered the Bishop's letter and asked the Minister for a copy of any colonial legislation dealing with liaisons between white men and native women, but none was passed in Papua.

What was passed was legislation to provide for the maintenance and care of 'Certain Children', an Act with the short title of Native (half-caste) Children Ordinance 1922. On a complaint being made that a person was father of a half-caste child who was neglected, the father could be summoned to appear before a magistrate and if the case was proven an affiliation order was made that he pay £26 a year for the maintenance of the child. Unless the man denied the allegation on oath, the mother's word was enough to establish paternity. Half-caste children could also be mandated, as native children could, to a mission, government station, ship's crew or a private person if they were under fourteen, had been convicted of an offence or were neglected. In the year 1926-7, seven European men were served with affiliation orders in respect of nine deserted half-caste children.

The 1921 Commonwealth census reported a total half-caste population for Papua as ninety-one males and sixty-seven females, with thirteen males and seven females in Port Moresby, but as most of the children of unions between Papuan women and white men lived with their mothers in the villages and, as Papuans were not counted in the census,

19

this figure would not have included those children. The count in the *Annual Report* for 1915-16 gave a Papuan total of half-castes as 341, of whom 191 were from the Central Division and 231 were children. This seems a more realistic picture.

Despite the figures in the *Annual Report*, however they were obtained, it was possible for white people to deny that liaisons between black women and white men were common in Papua. Correspondence in the pages of the *Bulletin* during 1926 demonstrates two white male views on miscegenation. The film 'White Cargo' was screening in Sydney which caused 'Bouragi' to write attacking it as a travesty of the South Seas Australian. 'The most easy-going Briton in savage lands had a contempt for the occasional maintainer of a native concubine, even if he has attained some standing in the community, and the feeling is, happily just as strong among Australians in Papua.'[50] 'Coconut' and 'Feng Shui' took issue with him, one to say that the number of half-castes in the Northern Territory and Queensland disproved his contention about Australians and the other to give the cynical white man's view of these liaisons. 'If he is so disposed the newcomer acquires a wife by purchase from her parents. She improves his domestic economy out of sight and is satisfied with a modest pension when her unobtrusive ministry is over. Often he goes and returns with a white wife when he can afford her, and his moral degeneration isn't noticed by his neighbours.'[51]

Sexual relations between black men and white women were considered so outside the bounds of possibility that, whereas in the Northern Territory Aboriginals Ordinance of 1918, a 'half-caste' was defined as any person who was the off-spring of parents 'one but not both of whom is an aboriginal', the Papuan Ordinance of 1922 defined a half-caste as 'the off-spring of a European father and a mother not wholly European'. This did not mean that the child of a European woman and a man not wholly of European descent was not defined as a half-caste; it meant that it was inconceivable.

Early residents recollect liaisons between black men or youths and white girls or women, but as none was publicly acknowledged, there is only rumour to support the recollections. Whatever the truth, no white girl married a black man until well after World War II. Even the most permissive of the white parent-rulers of Papua—or those who were counted so by the more patriarchal—were shocked and frightened by any suggestion of sexual connection between black men and white women.

It was partly a matter of class. Whites in Papua were mostly plain Australians, but all were in a higher social class than any Papuans; all whites were masters of black servants. And quite apart from their difference in colour these were servants such as few Australians except outback station owners had dealt with since the days of assigned convicts. Papuan servants were for the most part indentured and so tied to the job for two or three years—as well as protected— by the Provisions of the Native Labour Ordinance under whose Regulations it was an offence not only to desert and break the contract, but also not to show 'ordinary diligence in the performance of any work assigned'. They were also tied by the fact that their wages were often paid in a lump sum at the end of the specified period, usually at the end of the year, and unless the Commissioner for Native Affairs authorised payment of an 'advance' the servant had no money. The place and proportions of payment were stated in the contract of service and the method of payment could not be varied 'even with the consent of the native'. A device to protect employees from unscrupulous employers and to ensure that they finished their period of employment with a lump sum of money, it effectively tied men to their masters. There was no fixed minimum wage for any native employee and, although plantation and other labourers were given Sunday off under the Regulations, domestic servants were specifically excluded from this holiday. Nor was there a ration scale for domestic servants who were to be 'supplied with sufficient food as required'. Servants were physically chastised for wrong-doing. When H. L. Griffin was Acting Resident Magistrate of the Central Division in 1907, the seven white women of Port Moresby made many complaints about cheeky house servants. Griffin told the women to send each offending 'boy' to his office with a chit explaining the

21

circumstances of his misdemeanour, whereupon he would make a ruling that the 'boy' was under fourteen and send him to the gaol for 'six to ten cuts with a birch from Jimmy the gaoler'. Under the Native Regulations of 1908, one regulation provided that in the case of a person not over fourteen, the court could have him whipped in the presence of the court. 'The effect was electrical', wrote Griffin, and several years later ladies were heard to say that 'the only time we had really decent house boys was when Mr Griffin was acting as Resident Magistrate here'.[52] Griffin was dismissed for illegally shooting birds of paradise, but long after he had gone masters and mistresses treated their Papuan servants in a far more high and heavy-handed manner than people at the time treated servants in Australian towns. In 1926, L. T. Sefton, manager of Koitakinumu plantation, committee member of the Chamber of Commerce and founder of the Papua Club, was fined for assaulting natives.

Employers administered a cuff and a kick to their servants, and if there had been provocation and provided that the blows were administered with the open hand and caused no serious damage, they were allowed as a legitimate way of correcting native servants. Among the complaints brought by indentured servants to the Native Affairs Department during March and April 1930 was one against a Port Moresby mistress who, during an argument with a servant—during which he threw a pail of rubbish over the kitchen floor—slapped his face. The servant in this case was told that he must not be 'insolent and cheeky to white women . . . and must do as he is told'.[53] Another common way of directing servants was to scream at them. Evelyn Cheeseman's description of the manageress of one of Moresby's two pubs reveals her to be a great screamer-manager.[54] Of course many masters had excellent and kindly relations with their servants, and some stayed with their masters for many years, but this depended on the character of the employer.

Papuans were held to belong to an inferior race by even very enlightened Europeans. The fact that they were all servants while Europeans were all masters caused many to see the inferiority as proven, and made the prospect of liaison between black and white even more repellent. The belief that a woman is defiled by sexual relations—while a man is only demeaned—together with the prospect of her producing a mixed-race child, added a special dimension to male repulsion and to female fear.

So much did the white population regard itself as above and outside any relations with Papuans that the Royal Commissioners in 1906 'could not fail to notice the strong feeling with which the majority of the white population regarded possible arrest by one of the armed constabulary'. When Monckton recalled his capture of Joe O'Brien, 'one of the two greatest blackguards and all-round criminals' he had ever met,[55] a man who had raped village women, burnt villagers' huts, shot a village constable and stolen £1000 of gold from Whitten Bros, he told of how he and his armed native constables confronted O'Brien. 'You need not have brought those blank [sic] bastards', called O'Brien, 'don't let a nigger put the irons on me.' Monckton obliged. J. McDonald, head jailer, Scotsman and pillar of the Ela Protestant Church in the 1920s, tried at a church meeting to prevent a group of Papuans—who were in the main cooks of the congregation—from using the church for their own service. The Papuan service was to be at a different time from the European, but he said he would leave the church if Papuans were allowed to use it.[56]

In 1933, when the Government arranged English classes at the European school for the twelve Papuan Medical Assistants selected to go to Sydney for further training, 'the parents rose in their wrath and said that their children should never be contaminated by going to a building where natives had been'.[58]

'White prestige' dictated, even to the most excellent and humane of government officers, that the blacks who were ruled and the whites who ruled them ought to keep a proper distance from each other. Ivan Champion forbade R. L. Bannon, who was accompanying him and the members of the American Sugar Commission on a patrol in the Rigo area, to sleep in the village constable's house. 'I pointed out that I did not approve of a white man travelling with a Government Officer sleeping with one of his village constables', he wrote in his patrol report.[59] The effect of Bannon's behaviour was soon experienced, continued Champion. A few days later, at Hula, his cookboy was accidentally bumped into by Bannon. The cookboy 'cheekily' asked Bannon if he had any eyes in his head. Bannon let it pass. 'I did not', wrote Champion, 'as it happened to be my own boy. Had it been any other I should not have taken any notice. Bannon deserved it. We often get a wail about the natives' disrespect for us, but none about the whiteman's disrespect for himself.'

For a white woman or girl to fall in love with, or form a sexual liaison with, a lowly Papuan servant was a great blow to white prestige. Sexual self-doubts might easily worry the minds of husbands and fathers confronted daily by totally unfamiliar black male servants and these doubts, when added to a belief in the greater potency of black men, provided the basis for fear of sexual attack. Where every white woman is a Great Mother and every black man, therefore, a respectful son, there is another powerful reason why touching a white woman was forbidden.

Until the twenties it was rare to find any statement from white men about the danger to their women and children from sexual attack by Papuans. 'Morobe', writing in the *Bulletin*, looked back in 1926 to the good days when 'the European woman stood on a plane so infinitely superior to the native that for him even to think of her carnally was an impiety terrifying to the imagination'.[60] In Port Moresby servants had the opportunity to gratify their curiosity and sexual urges by peeping at, touching, stroking or attempting to lie with the white women of the town. The freedom from village restraints and the anonymity which Papuan house servants encountered in the town, compared with those other places where white women might be met, enabled some now and again to take the opportunity. From the middle 1920s, the threat, real and imagined, of these actions became an increasing preoccupation of the white residents of Port Moresby and other towns. Some of the reasons for this may be discovered in an examination of the town which they had built on the shores of Moresby harbour.

Two   The white man's town

PORT MORESBY was an Australian colonial town. It is possible to examine quite precisely the demography of the town in this period because, in 1921 and again in 1933, all inhabitants of Papua except the Papuans were counted as part of the Census of the Commonwealth of Australia. As Port Moresby was one of the census districts, the statistical information published in the census reports, added to descriptive material from observers, makes it possible to anatomise the social structure of the town. Similar sources make it possible to examine the character of the other two Australian colonial towns, Darwin and Rabaul. Darwin had been administered by the Commonwealth Government since 1911 when it took over that task from the South Australian Government. Rabaul had been a German town until 1914 and, when Australian civil administration began in May 1921, it was under the eye of the Permanent Mandates Commission of the League of Nations. Each was a tropical outpost, far from central government, in a territory administered by a local official with wide powers. Each was an isolated frontier town where white men came to make a sort of life for themselves on the edge of a country containing a population of indigenous blacks. All three towns were administered by white Australians, most of whom shared the same basic assumptions outlined in chapter 1; they shared other characteristics too, but Port Moresby had also some distinctive ones. Looking at the similarities and differences between Port Moresby and the other two outposts can help generally to characterise Port Moresby society and may help in particular to illuminate the subject of this work.

The Port Moresby census district embraced a larger area than the Port Moresby town, reaching from Gaile (on some maps, Gaire) twenty-three crowflight miles south-east of the town, to Redscar Head, twenty-two and a half crowflight miles west. But, in the preliminary table from the census, which was published in the Papuan *Annual Report* for 1921, the year the census was held, figures are broken down into the different areas within the census district. These figures show that 59 per cent of the total population 'exclusive of full blood Papuan aboriginals' that is 335 persons—and 64 per cent of the European (used in the census tables as a euphemism for white) population or 313 persons lived in the town. There is a discrepancy of twenty-five between the total population figure shown in the preliminary table and the figure which appeared in 1925 in the final publication of the census.

The Port Moresby non-Papuan community in 1921 was very small: 577 men, women and children. In Rabaul there were 1350 and in Darwin 1399.

Statistically Port Moresby was a very masculine place. The ratio of males to every hundred females over the whole of its non-Papuan population was 203, but in some of the adult age groups it was still higher. It was much higher again in Rabaul. Darwin was less masculine than Port Moresby in younger and older age groups, but more masculine in the twenty-five to thirty-four groups. The most masculine community of the three was Rabaul, where in the adult age groups there was a spectacular oversupply of males.

An excess of males over females was a feature of all North Queensland and the Northern Territory in 1921, and of all pioneering places. Another mark of Port Moresby's pioneer character was the number of men without wives, either unmarried men or men whose wives and families lived elsewhere. Hubert Murray was one, as was G. A. Loudon, Manager of the British New Guinea Development Co. The *Courier* of 18 September 1925 reported the return to Port Moresby of Mrs G. A. Loudon 'after an absence of eighteen months spent in Europe'. Of Port Moresby's 320 males over fourteen years old, 170 or 53 per cent were unmarried (that is never married, widowers or divorced men); 150 were married, but forty-eight of these did not have their wives in Port Moresby. In this the three towns were very similar: 54 per cent of Rabaul males over fifteen and 54 per cent of Darwin males over fifteen had no wives.

The unmarried non-Papuan males of Port Moresby had

very few unmarried females to choose from. There were only twenty-five unmarried females over fifteen in the census district, thirty-one when the widows and divorcees were counted in. Darwin males were better provided with females: for 402 unmarried men there were 102 unmarried females; and Rabaul men had the smallest number: for 535 unmarried males there were only eighty-nine unmarried females over fifteen to choose from.

There were only 190 females in the Port Moresby census district, of whom fifty-seven were under fifteen; of those over fifteen, 102 out of the 133 were married; of the thirty-one who were not, twenty-five had never been married and six were widows.

The Port Moresby community was predominantly white, Anglo-Saxon, male and Protestant. In the 1921 census, citizens had to state if they were 'of European race' or, if not European, to 'state what race'. European was defined in terms of what was *not* European and examples were given of 'a person of other than European race, i.e. Aboriginal, Chinese, Japanese, Hindu, etc.' These persons had to state the names of their races in full. In the case of people of mixed race the letters H.C.—for half-caste—were to be added, for example, H.C. Aboriginal, H.C. Chinese, etc. Those classed as half-caste had 'European blood to the extent of one half'. No off-spring of a mixed European and non-European union might call himself H.C. European. Whereas the off-spring of a Chinese-Papuan union or a Polynesian-Chinese union might choose which 'half' to belong to, the off-spring of a European-Chinese union or a European-Papuan union might not. White was made non-white by the mixture; black was not made non-black. Thus in Port Moresby, 84 per cent of non-Papuan males and 78 per cent of non-Papuan females were Europeans, while in Rabaul only 27 per cent of males and 20 per cent of females were Europeans and in Darwin 60 per cent of males and 64 per cent of females were Europeans. In the sense that European really meant 'white', Port Moresby, Papua, was a far more white-Australian place than Darwin, Australia.

The largest number of non-Europeans in both Rabaul and Darwin were the Chinese: 86 per cent of non-European males in Rabaul were Chinese[1] and 73 per cent of non-European women; in Darwin the Chinese males made up 49 per cent of the non-European males and the females 26 per cent. There were one Chinese man and one Chinese woman living in Port Moresby in 1921 who together with forty-eight males of other non-European races and thirty-four females and the fourteen male and seven female half-castes made up the total non-European population.

The Port Moresby white Europeans *were* the town, and made its institutions on the basis of their own whiteness. When the government decided to open a school in 1909, the only barrier was racial. 'What kind of a school is it to be?' asked a member of the Legislative Council. It was to be 'an undenominational school. Children to be of European parentage only', replied the Treasurer, H. W. Champion.

The Port Moresby population was more British by birth than the population of Darwin: 53 per cent of Port Moresby males had been born in Australasia and 21 per cent in the British Isles, making a total of 74 per cent. Port Moresby non-Papuan women were less British born than their husbands: 66 per cent of them had been born in Australasia or the British Isles.

In Darwin, 65 per cent of males had been born in Australasia or the British Isles. In Rabaul, only 27 per cent of the male population was born in Australasia, the British Isles or New Guinea, while 54 per cent had been born in China.

Very few of those who inhabited either colonial town had been born there. Sixty-seven Port Moresby males and fifty-four females (16 and 28 per cent respectively) and seventy-six Rabaul males and sixty-seven females (7 and 24 per cent) had been born in Papua or the Mandated Territory.

British and white, the non-Papuan population of Port Moresby was necessarily more Christian than that of either Rabaul or Darwin. Eighty-eight per cent (342 out of 387) of Port Moresby males and 96 per cent (182 out of 190) of Port Moresby females said they were Christians, compared with 62 per cent of Darwin males and 79 per cent of Darwin females, and only 36 per cent of Rabaul males and 39 per cent of Rabaul females. The figure for Australia as a whole was closer to that of Port Moresby; 96 per cent of Australian males and 99 per cent of females claimed to be Christian in 1921.

Of these Christians, most were Protestants; only 17 per cent of male Christians were Catholic, Roman or other. But 30 per cent of female Christians were Roman Catholics. In Rabaul 28 per cent of Christian males and 41 per cent of Christian females were Catholic, and in Australia as a whole, the proportion was 21 per cent of both male and female Christians. The much higher proportion of female to male Roman Catholics in Port Moresby may be explained by the arrival in 1921 of the Order of the Sacred Heart to establish a convent and a school. Mixed race girls, who were brought in from country areas to board with the nuns, would have increased the figure for Roman Catholic females.[2]

Less Catholic than Australia as a whole, the Port Moresby males harboured some anti-Catholic feeling, especially focused on the Catholic Lieutenant-Governor, Hubert Murray. Atlee Hunt, Secretary of the Department of Home and Territories, in correspondence with Joseph King of the London Missionary Society, learned of the missionary's fears 'that . . . the residents of Yule Island are anxious for ecclesiastical reasons to see Mr Murray in the position'.[3] The correspondence between Staniforth Smith and Atlee Hunt in 1911-13 reveals that both men, especially Staniforth Smith, were hostile to Catholics, and that both were very conscious that Murray was a Catholic and an Irish nationalist. Murray was aware of it. 'The anti-Catholic feeling is very strong out here', he wrote to his brother Gilbert in 1922.[4]

In 1921, most of the 320 male breadwinners in Port Moresby census district were planters or civil servants. The professional category was very large compared with Rabaul and Darwin and with Australia as a whole. The residents of Port Moresby were government employees, planters, merchants, traders, clerks, missionaries and miners. There was no hard and fast division and up to the end of World War I it was common for a man to move from 'commercial' to 'government', or vice versa, or even to be in both at the same time, though this last declined during the Murray administration.

Port Moresby females were mostly dependants, being either children or married women. There were only twenty-eight female breadwinners in 1928 who made up 14 per cent of the total female population.

Only 3 per cent of Port Moresby breadwinners were employers of labour, 10 per cent worked on their own accounts, and the largest percentage of breadwinners—73 per cent—were on wages and salaries. Nine per cent were unemployed. This was much the same division as in Rabaul in 1921. In Rabaul, 2 per cent of male breadwinners (which takes in everyone except the indigenous population and includes the Chinese) were employers, 15 per cent worked on their own account, and 76 per cent were on wages and salaries while 3 per cent were unemployed. There was more unemployment in Darwin, where 23 per cent of male bread-winners were not employed, 4 per cent were employers, 15 per cent worked on their own account and 54 per cent were on wages and salaries.

The non-Papuan population of Port Moresby remained small during the 1920s. Over the twelve years between the 1921 and 1933 censuses, it increased by only fifty-one persons, or 8 per cent. This was a smaller increase than those in Rabaul and Darwin, where the increases were 16 per cent and 12 per cent respectively.

Port Moresby was still a very small outpost. What had changed, during these years, was the number of women and the proportion of women to men. There were ninety-three more females (about eighty-six of whom would have been white) living in the Port Moresby census division than there had been in 1921. Now the population was 54 per cent male and 45 per cent female, whereas in 1921 67 per cent of the population had been male. Women certainly did arrive in Port Moresby in the years after 1921.[5]

There were similar increases in the non-indigenous female population of Rabaul and Darwin. The most spectacular increase in the number of women was in Rabaul, 107 per cent increase; the post-war settlement after civil administration was established no doubt encouraged men to bring wives. The increase in the female population of Darwin was 36 per cent on the 1921 figure; that of Port Moresby was 49 per cent. In all three towns, as amenities were provided, more women found it possible to settle.

An even higher proportion of Port Moresby's males now worked in professional, administrative and clerical occupations than in 1921: 31 per cent of all male breadwinners. In 1933, 24 per cent of male breadwinners worked in commercial occupations compared with 13 per cent in 1921, but those working in primary industry declined to 10 per cent, a decline which may be accounted for by the decrease from forty-six to twenty-two men working in agricultural pursuits (the failure of some plantations during the economic crisis?) and the complete disappearance of miners from Port Moresby census district when the New Guinea Copper Company's works on the shores of Bootless Inlet closed down in 1927 after years of financial troubles. In Rabaul, the proportion of men in each category of occupation changed very little. Men in Darwin continued to work at the same sort of occupations as in 1921 and roughly in the same proportions.

In the early 1920s, all three towns were very high in masculinity and remained so, but in all three there was an increase of females during the mid-1920s. The lack of women has been suggested as a cause of sexual attack. Clearly it was not so in Papua for despite the great lack of women, no case of a European, Asian or other non-Papuan man attacking a non-Papuan woman or girl came before the Central Court during this period. On the other hand, very many cases of Papuan men attacking Papuan women or girls did come before the Central Court.

Port Moresby, as we have seen, was similar to Darwin and Rabaul in many ways. It was however peculiar in several important respects. It was a very small community, less than half the size of Rabaul or Darwin and so more vulnerable in its alien environment. It was far more a white man's town than either Rabaul or Darwin and it had no Chinese community to act as a buffer between it and the blacks, to divert black resentment, to provide a complication to the whites' notions of their own superiority. Consequently the confrontation of the two groups was clearer, the need to keep apart greater, and the pressures towards unity of the whole non-Papuan community more powerful. The residents of Port Moresby were not only more white, they were more British, Christian and Protestant; and all these factors added to their cohesiveness in the face of an alien black environment.

Port Moresby was peculiar too in that the non-Papuan population divided more clearly into two groups—commercial and civil service—than the other two towns; the trend was marked in 1921 and became even more marked by 1933.

Finally, only Port Moresby had Hubert Murray. There was no other 'Australian pro-Consul'; no Administrator whose personality was so strong, who was at once so intellectual and so purposeful or so aloof from the rank and file of residents. Murray's policies were more clearly stated than those of the German-based Mandate administration, more humane and more based on law. He insisted that all regulation of natives be legal and he forbade summary punishment. But this threw more of the burden of protection of the white population on to the government. For if the white population had to be protected—and everyone agreed that it had—and if one could not take the law into one's own hands immediately, then the government could not afford to be slack in its responsibilities towards the safety of white residents. Murray was often attacked for being too lax and too benevolent, both faults being seen as a direct result of his native policy. 'The Papuan administration prides itself on its native policy, which largely consists in letting Brown Brother have an open go, and fining employers', was how many commercial and planting people saw it.[6]

Port Moresby was a small white community, united in its whiteness against the blacks, divided, almost solely, for or against the government as personified by the Lieutenant-Governor. These features of the town must be borne in mind if we are to understand the coming of the White Women's Protection Ordinance.

Papuans called the area on which the town was built 'Ela'. The British founders named the town officially 'Granville'. 'Port Moresby' was the name used by Australian postal officials and then taken up by the white Australian inhabitants. They called it simply 'Port', which suggested not a place to live in, but a place to arrive at and leave from. It had been developed on the saddle between two hills of the

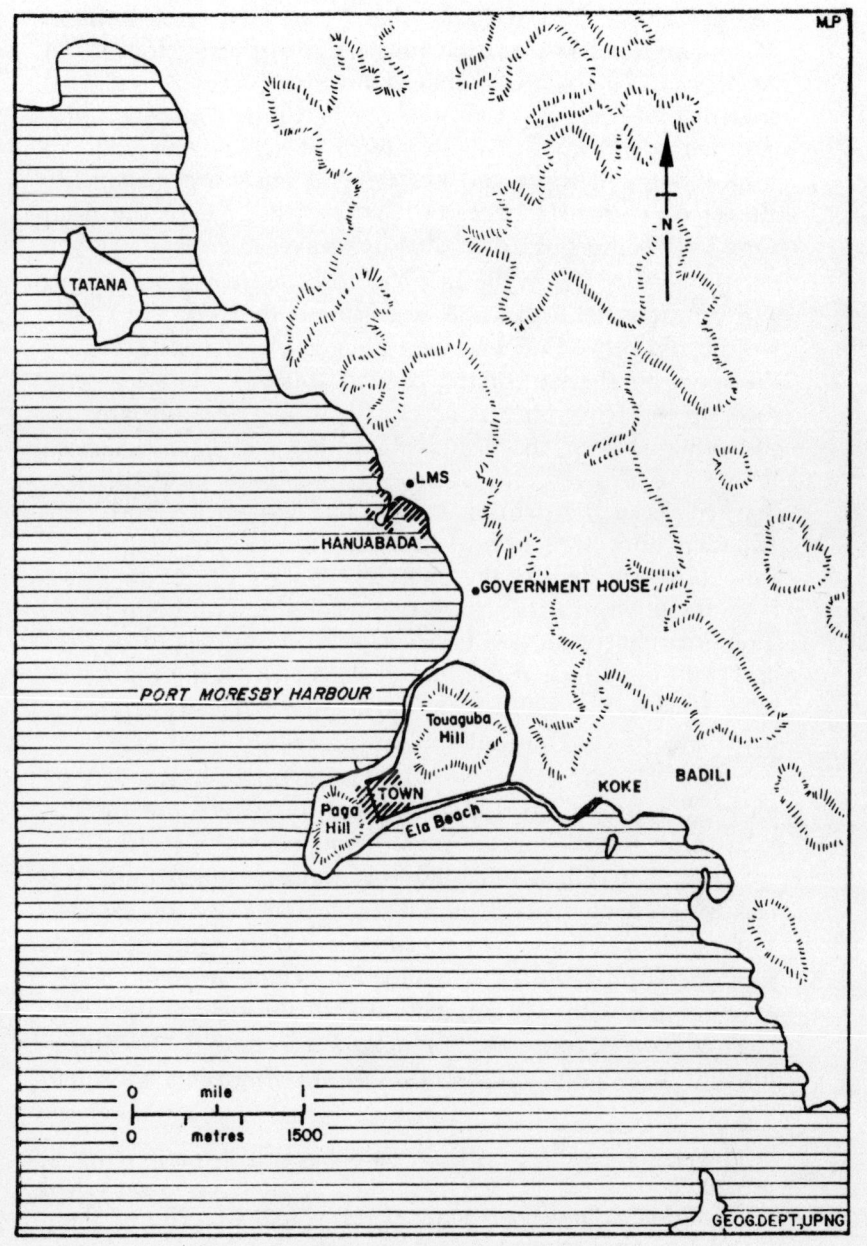

Port Moresby and its environs

peninsula one and a half miles away from the London Missionary Society's mission house, Government House, and Andrew Goldie's store—the first three places of colonial settlement—because Commissioner John Douglas who planned the town during his term of office from 1886 to 1888 thought it wiser and healthier to build away from the cluster of Papuan villages on the coastline where the dead were still being buried in shallow graves.

From the days of the British Protectorate, the native and white residential areas were segregated. In 1884, the trader Goldie was moved off his site among the native villages into the town on the site of the present Burns Philp store, and took up residence on fifty acres of land at Badili, an area on the other side of the peninsula which had been acquired before the Protectorate. From then on, land in Badili was marked as a residential centre for Papuans, South Sea Islanders and other non-whites.[7] Papuan labour compounds were built at Badili; the gaol was moved to nearby Koke from the town in 1913. All were outside the town boundaries. The only exception was the Native Hospital, begun in 1913 and built out to sea at the foot of Paga Hill on the Ela Beach side. During the 1920s agitation to move it away from the town was pretty constant but unsuccessful.

By 1921 the town boundaries were Lawes Road, Port Road, Ela Beach Road and Cuthbertson Street and on this hilly plot the European town had grown. No visitor or coloniser had much affection for it, Englishmen and Australians uniting in condemnation. It reminded the Special Commissioner of the *Sydney Morning Herald* in 1921 of 'a superior mining town'.[8] 'A collection of hot tin roofs', wrote a visitor in 1920, 'My Papuans rolled the luggage up a corrugated iron street to the corrugated iron hotel.'[9] 'Utilitarianism is writ large on everything', an English visitor had written in 1914.

> The centre 'road' . . . is lined on either side by various stores, banks and hotels, all hideous in their bareness, every one raised on piles and built of wood and corrugated iron. Burns Philp and Co's buildings dominate the port . . . The Germans do these things better than we do . . .[10]

In this respect, she would not have found the town of the 1920s an improvement.

Everyone remarked on the lack of shade and gardens. Port Moresby has an average rainfall of about forty inches, all of it in one season. A constant water supply depended on storing water during the wet season. As the residents held it the Lieutenant-Governor's responsibility to provide them with water, and as the Lieutenant-Governor—with very little money to spend on the whole of Papua—believed that the residents should provide their own tanks, not much progress was made. There was a government reservoir on one of the peaks from which water was sold in times of drought. Water tickets were issued, printed and dated so that a fair share was ensured, but the government's failure to provide a piped water supply to the town remained one of the residents' chief complaints. H. W. Champion, the Government Secretary, planned and executed what beauty and shade there were in the town and went about after work watering the street plants, but he had to ask the residents not to send their servants to collect flowers from the street. 'The trees are becoming torn about,' he wrote, 'and branches are broken off without any regard for the trees whatsoever; they are usually denuded of all blooms and present an unsightly appearance.'[11] It was hard to persuade the residents of Port Moresby to take enough interest in the town to beautify it; nor did the government consider that building beautiful colonial towns in the German manner was the Australian way, though Australians could build very attractive tropical towns, as Cairns shows.

By 1925, the town had government-installed electric light, street lighting and power; a hospital for Europeans, another for natives, a dentist who manned his chair alternately in Port Moresby and Samarai, the other main white centre of Papua on an island off the coast in the Eastern Division; four general stores, two banks; two pubs; government offices, a cafe, a boarding house and a mail service to Australia every five weeks. Although perhaps only a romantic artist could see the town fitting happily into the 'primitive Arcadia' which was Papua, its natural setting was spectacularly beautiful and it was not a much more difficult town to live in than many a far north Queensland town.

It was a poor and impermanent looking town. Neither commerce nor government built fine substantial buildings with style and character. Domestic building was better, being the North Queensland-style tropical bungalow with wide verandahs, built of imported materials. Papuans' building materials, like their food and clothing and ways of life were too alien, unsophisticated, uncomfortable and impermanent for the non-Papuan residents to adopt in their town. They did not enjoy sago and yams, the staple diet of the local Papuans, and with a five-weekly boat from Australia were not forced to eat them, but subsisted mainly on tinned food, unless they were lucky enough to employ a 'shooting boy' who brought in fresh wallaby.

Home was close enough for residents to visit frequently, it was just 'south'. The *Papuan Courier* of 25 September 1925 listed those leaving Port on the *Morinda* for Cairns and Sydney as thirteen to Cairns and twenty-two to Sydney. Returning passengers, listed in the *Courier* of 19 February 1926, numbered twenty-six returning to Port, seven to Bootless Inlet and twenty-one to Samarai. And in 1936 a Guinea Airways plane which had taken off from Wau with seven passengers, landed at Port Moresby, collected two more and took off for the Melbourne Cup. The return fare was £80 reported the *Rabaul Times* on 30 October. Government employes received vacation leave of six weeks in one year or six months in four years. After six years' service, they received long leave of six months on full pay or twelve months on half pay and after fifteen years in government service received furlough of six months on full pay or twelve months on half. Many children went 'south' for their schooling and at the end of the year the wharf was thronged with excited mothers awaiting the arrival of children for their midsummer vacation from southern schools.

In 1921 there was no social column in the *Papuan Courier* but by 1934 a local column conducted by 'Prudence' and a syndicated one by 'Miss Mary Tallis' appeared regularly. Miss Mary Tallis's piece for 1 January 1934 was headed 'The First Days of Summer'—although all year is summer in Port Moresby—and gave advice on clothing. The fashion-conscious liked to keep in touch with the current fashions at home, so no one could have thought ridiculous the following advice given in April: 'If you like the sort of fur necklaces which hang down in front and make a ruff round the back, pin them gently to your coat'.

For the residents, the amusements and the social life were made, like the houses, after the Australian pattern, with a Library Institute, a Turf Club, a Cricket Club, a Golf Club, a Returned Soldiers' League and a social club which did have a local name, the Betel Social Club. The only new sport in Papua was canoe racing, run by the Port Moresby Aquatic Club. Papuan dug-out canoes, with sails, owned by Hanuabadan villagers, crewed and coxed by Papuans, were captained by white residents who paid a fixed rate for the use of the canoe and to each crew member per race. In 1925 racing was suspended since the villagers demanded 2/6 a race for coxes and 1/6 for crew and the members of the Aquatic Club refused to pay the new fee. In the following year, although one member counselled standing firm until the natives came forward to man the canoes under the old 'or even less liberal terms' and another that 'natives be eliminated and Europeans endeavour to arrange crews between themselves' the Club agreed to the villagers' demands, amended its rules to allow payment of the new fees, and racing began again. Except when captaining the Hanuabadan canoes, the white residents engaged in the same recreations as people 'south'.

Much more than in Australian towns, the residents of Port Moresby were united simply by being white. Other distinctions faded in significance. All the European children of Port Moresby were invited to the Government House picnic or Christmas party; the Headquarters Officer of the Armed Native Constabulary invited the white residents of Port Moresby to be present at a display of his constabulary; all white adults who cared to dance went to the occasional dance at the Library Institute Hall; all white men could join the Chamber of Commerce and Residents' Association; all could take part in the amateur theatricals or the regular cricket match between teams whose names reflected the social composition of the town: Boarding House v. The Rest of the World; Government v. Commercial; Port Moresby v. Samarai.

What division there was among the white residents was that between 'government' and 'commercial', though a certain amount of class distinction was maintained in the Papua Club where the leaders of the planting and business community allowed only a few of the leading public servants to join them each afternoon. Formed just before World War I by T. L. Sefton, a planter from Koitakinumu in the hills close to Port Moresby, the club still exists. Its members were called 'the ablest colonials in the Pacific' by Dr S. M. Lambert, who came to Port Moresby in 1920 to run a campaign against hookworm,[12] and its presidents during this period were Arthur Jewell (1916-23), W. M. Strong (1924), G. A. Loudon (1925-7), T. L. Sefton (1928), H. W. Champion (1929) and R. T. Gore (1931-4). The office bearers of the Turf Club were mainly planters and leading businessmen, the only government office bearer being Staniforth Smith, the planters' friend, who long had been an opponent, and even enemy, of Murray.

The white wage and salary earners, being largely government employees, were not a class-conscious group. The only hint of class-consciousness in the *Papuan Courier* came from 'Employee', who wrote saying that since the Citizens' Committee was 'the direct representative of capital' because 'its chairman is an employer and the majority of its members are employers', it should 'change its name to the Employers' Federation . . . and the employees should form a Papuan Labour League'. But such a League was not formed and the only trade union which existed was the Public Service Association.

The salaries of Port Moresby's public servants were a source of discontent throughout the 1920s. Until 1920 there had been no classification of the service; the Lieutenant-Governor had received £1250, the Chief Judicial Officer £1000, the Government Secretary £700 and the Treasurer £600. Resident Magistrates received £475 and patrol officers £225. After classification, all salaries except those for the two top positions were improved. The Government Secretary's pay rose to £850, Resident Magistrates' to £570 and patrol officers' to £300. Public servants (except the Lieutenant-Governor) had to pay rent, at a rate of up to 10 per cent of their salaries except when occupying a native materials house, which was rent free.

At £1250, the Lieutenant-Governor's salary was the same as that of the Secretary of the Prime Minister's Department, but lower than that of the Secretary of the Department of the Treasury in the Commonwealth Public Service. Patrol officers and other outside men were paid at the same rate as clerks in the Commonwealth Department of Public Works, whose pay also included rent for their houses. The re-classification of the service which took place in 1926 produced more improvements, but in general all public servants, from the Lieutenant-Governor down, thought they should have received more—as their work was more complex and difficult—than those with whom they were rated equivalent in the Commonwealth Service. Among lesser members of the service there was also some resentment at the disparity between the salary of the Lieutenant-Governor and other officers, but on the whole the public servants were a united group who were loyal to the Lieutenant-Governor.

Traditional political affiliations were blurred as men were divided by their support for or opposition to the Lieutenant-Governor and his policies, a political division based primarily, though not exclusively, on the division between 'official' and 'commercial' employment. The commercial group believed that Murray did too little for European development. 'The fundamental sophistry', wrote the Planters' Association, 'which affects like a canker the whole system of Papuan administration by the Commonwealth is the apparent assumption that the possible accumulation of wealth by private individuals or corporations resulting from the work of development of the country is evil and must be prevented at all costs.'[13] The *Courier* carried in 1920 the revolutionary slogan 'No representation. No taxation.' and the paper constantly attacked the Lieutenant-Governor, sometimes for his own misdeeds, sometimes as the representative of a government which, from afar, made policies with no first-hand knowledge of Papua and had them rubber-stamped by a Legislative Council, the majority of whose members were official and the rest chosen by the Lieutenant-Governor, and which, in any case, could debate only bills initiated by the Lieutenant-Governor and on which he had a casting vote.

Dissatisfaction, reinforced by a hatred of Murray, erupted in 1920 in a series of public outcries. The residents wanted their voices heard more strongly in Melbourne, the temporary federal capital. As they had no confidence that the Lieutenant-Governor would speak in their interest, they met in January 1920, under the chairmanship of J. J. Hunter, manager of the Laloki copper mine, to discuss their lack of representation. The chairman's father, the *Papuan Courier* said ominously, had been at Eureka. They angrily proposed that the white residents of Papua should have direct representation in the federal parliament, and defeated an alternate proposal for elective representation in the Papuan Legislative Council. This tiny electorate set up a 'Citizens' Committee' to fight for the franchise, and the *Courier* put forward W. C. Bruce as its candidate for the post of Senator with voice but no vote.

More trouble broke out. The following month Murray made the tactless statement, in reply to an article criticising Papuan labour policy, that white tradesmen in Papua were 'very highly paid, and they are not very efficient, or, if they are, they soon cease to be from the influence of the climate'.[14] Malays and other Asians, he said, could work better in the climate and for less money, as German New Guinea showed. There Chinese artisans worked well and received seven shillings a day without rations, less than half the wages of Europeans. There was a tremendous fuss, which could have been more serious had not Murray's opponents overreached themselves. The residents' groups flew together to express their indignation. The R.S.L. said that it was not only 'casting a slur on returned men, but odiously compares them with Chinamen'. 'I cannot understand a white man saying such a thing', declaimed one enraged member. 'It is disgusting' said another.[15] Murray's conclusion, that Chinese nonetheless should continue to be excluded from Papua because their presence would give rise to a race problem and because they could easily enter Australia from there, was ignored.

The Citizens' Committee, which had become the leading anti-Murray body in the town, called a meeting for 15 March at which a motion was moved demanding an apology from the Lieutenant-Governor and notifying him that 'the boat leaves in a few days'.[16] Perhaps this sounded too much like rebellion, for an amendment, stating that His Excellency had lost the confidence of the white community and urging the Australian Government to appoint Staniforth Smith in his place, was carried by seventy-five votes to fifty-nine. Similar meetings were held in Samarai. (The Australian Government did not oblige and His Excellency remained.)

Later in 1920 there was another explosion. This time the occasion was the repeated disagreement within the government medical service between a newly arrived doctor, Mathews, and the rest of the Government Medical Officers. Drs Strong, Harse and Lambert (the visiting hookworm specialist) thought Mathews was mentally unbalanced. The arguments about the administration of the native hospital and about Mathews's prescriptions grew bitter, and were made public by Mathews. The Citizens' Committee championed Mathews against the administration and when he was finally sacked, welcomed him as an active member of the anti-Murray faction.

At one of the almost weekly public meetings called in this explosive year, citizens passed a motion calling for the removal of Murray, but it was passed by only thirteen votes to eleven, and there was some discontent among members who felt that the chairman, Captain Fitch, the manager of Steamships Trading Company, was behaving in a proprietorial and evasive manner when asked about the membership of the Committee. They moved that a proper Association with rules and officers elected by ballot be formed.

Before that could be done, Captain Fitch sent a telegram to King George V:

Persistent despotic and persecuting actions by Governor Murray leading to serious and dangerous uprising of white people in Papua. Repeated demands for enquiry and redress by Commonwealth both ignored. Respectfully request His Majesty to take immediate action which honour and integrity Empire demands.[17]

41

It was too much. The meeting which had been called originally to discuss rules for the new Citizens' Association proved to be much more exciting. The public servants turned out in a body. When Captain Fitch tried to close the meeting before it could discuss the telegram to the King, it became clear that he had sent it quite on his own initiative. He was howled down and left the chair. In the uproar that followed, it turned out that the Committee had never heard of the telegram which had lain on the table during the whole of the last committee meeting, but had not been brought up! In his defence, Captain Fitch said that 'as many as twenty men had visited him and suggested that they should employ drastic militant tactics to secure their aim.' But he would neither name any of them nor explain why he had not reported their actions. The final resolution which the meeting passed repudiated the telegram as the work of 'unauthorised persons' instead of the work of 'irresponsible agitators' which had been the first version. Partly because Captain Fitch and his group had acted so stupidly and partly because there were so many public servants in the town, the forces of law and order and calm had triumphed. 'Those present dispersed after singing the National Anthem.'[18]

The chance to dismiss Murray had gone, but those who had urged 'drastic militant tactics' employed them soon after, significantly in the name of white women, whose chief part in the whole sordid case was to be pawns in the campaign against Murray. When Mathews left the government health service he had, as a matter of government policy, forfeited the right to use the hospital for private patients. His patients could from then on either be treated by him at home or they could go to the hospital and be treated by the doctor on duty. The Citizens' Committee took up this matter and called another meeting on 8 November from which a deputation, led by Captain Fitch, was sent to the Government Secretary, urging that Mathews be permitted to use the hospital for his patients as he 'was in great demand and . . . women have particular faith in him.'[19] The government's position was clearly explained to the deputation. Murray left for Australia early in December leaving Judge Herbert, the Acting Administrator, to face the next round of attacks.

The first female pawn was a nun, Sister Pascal, suffering from weakness and malaria. She became ill on Christmas night 1920, and would have no other than Mathews. Father Bailey rang Herbert to say that the Citizens' Association was taking up Sister Pascal's case and that he did not like it at all. Herbert favoured allowing Mathews to use the hospital but at the insistence of the Australian Government he issued a statement saying that Dr Mathews's patients must be treated according to the rules of the hospital and attended by hospital staff.

There had been two maternity cases pending among the wives of the deputation in support of Dr Mathews. The first was Mrs Skelly, wife of E. C. Skelly, Secretary of the Citizens' Committee and employee of Captain Fitch in Steamships Trading Co. When she came into labour early in 1921, her husband brought her to the hospital and began the final engagement in a battle which had been raging for several months. The Matron rang Dr Mathews, who immediately rang number 40 (Steamships Trading Co.) and reported to Fitch that Mrs Skelly was at the hospital and that he was going up, while a crowd of people, about fifteen or sixteen, had gone already. But when they arrived Dr Mathews and his supporters found their way barred by a row of twenty-two citizens who had been sworn in as special constables by Resident Magistrate O'Malley and were sitting ready to defend the hospital against the invader, authorised to use force to meet force. Two residents, Bannon and J. J. Hunter, had heard the talk of storming the hospital and each reported it to the European constable. One of the special constables was E. A. James, later to become owner and editor of the *Papuan Courier*. The Matron's disloyal actions and the names of the instigators were made known to His Excellency when the Chief Postmaster, who had been listening to everyone's telephone, sent in his report of the morning's calls.[20]

But what had the makings of a residents' revolt against the colonial administration fizzled out in words. Mrs Skelly had her baby without Dr Mathews and the militant anti-Murray residents had overreached themselves. The Australian Government supported the colonial administration's policy on the hospital, even insisting on it when the Acting

Administrator would have given in to the residents' pressure. In Port Moresby the death in 1922 of W. C. Bruce, editor of the *Courier* and determined enemy of Hubert Murray, removed a powerful and effective pen from the hands of the anti-Murray faction. 'Everything is quiet here' wrote Murray in December to Hugh Mahon, a former Federal member for Kalgoorlie and a fellow supporter of Ireland.[21] Murray received a knighthood in the New Year's Honours of 1925 and the pride of producing a local knight for the time being tempered the residents' hostility to him. Murray received the warm and unanimous tribute of the Chamber of Commerce and Residents' Association, the new body formed after Fitch's telegram had finished the old Citizens' Committee in 1920, and the sender of that telegram was quoted in the *Papuan Courier* of 30 January 1925 as saying that 'after a real [*sic*] long tenure of office in such an outpost of Empire as this the distinction given to His Excellency was richly deserved'. In September 1925 Murray had succeeded, after several years of representations, in having the provisions of the Navigation Act removed from Papua.[22] Under these provisions, which had been applied to Papua in 1921, when the prices of rubber and copra were already falling, all products bound for and from Papua had to go on Australian ships and first through Sydney, whatever their ultimate destination. This increased the cost of Papuan products on the world market and increased costs to Papuan consumers. 'The rice we purchase' wrote Murray 'will continue to go south past our door to Sydney, and must be trans shipped and sent north again to Port Moresby.'[23] This pleased only Burns Philp, the subsidised shipping line, whose rates, said Murray, were probably the highest ocean freights in the world. Murray's success removed some of the rancour against him for a time, and in 1926, when the Australian Government recognised the needs of its Papuan producers and introduced a system of bounties on tropical crops, Murray was able to report with great pleasure that exports had exceeded imports in that year. But it was too late, the economy did not recover and the Port Moresby white community remained discontented during this period.

They inhabited their tiny white demesne in what they

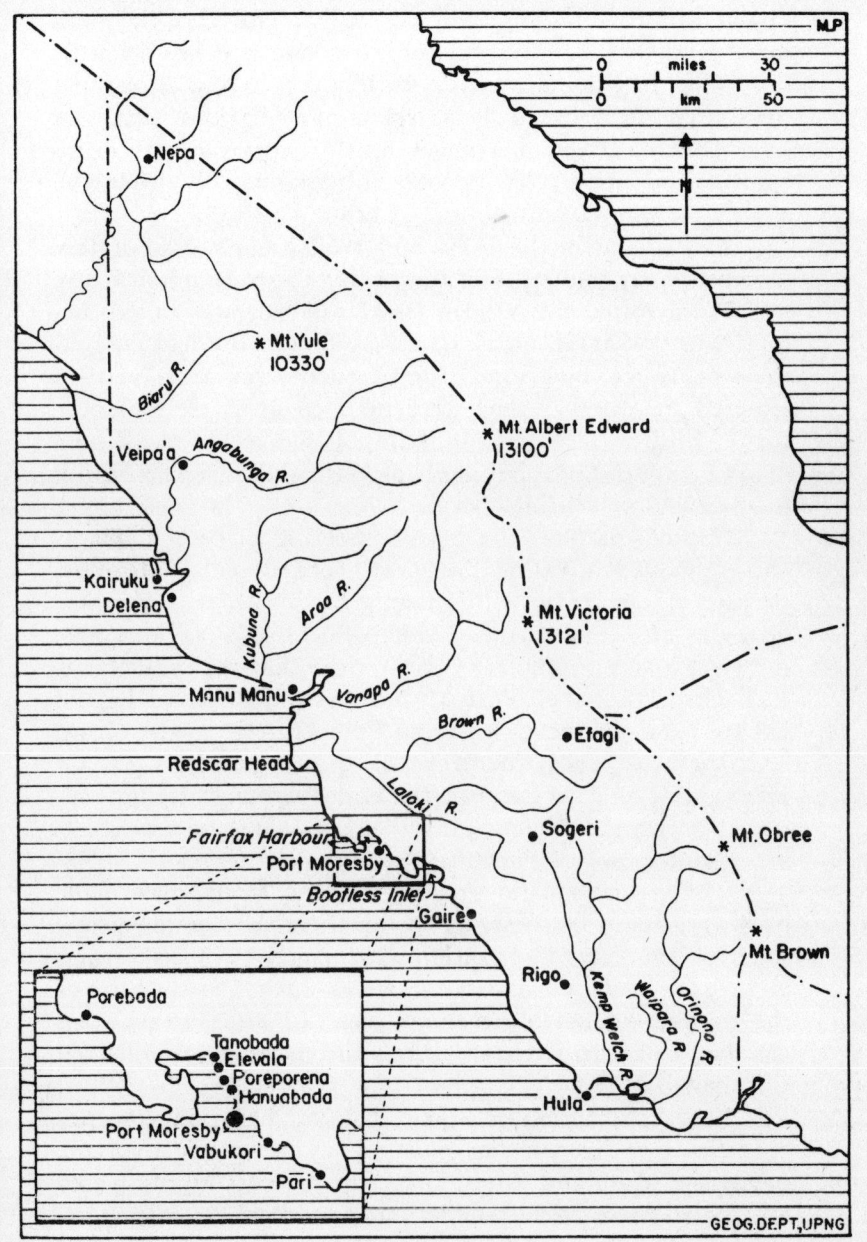

The Central Division

saw as a hostile and alien Papuan world. The town they had made was, they believed, a European one and not a native one. They had few relations with Papuans except as servants or simple flock or lowly workers, no relations with the neighbouring Papuan villages and in general very little information about the Papuan inhabitants, of either the Village or the Town who milled around them.

As Papuans in the 1920s and 1930s were not accurately or consistently counted, it is impossible to say even how many people inhabited the Village (as Hanuabada was called) before World War II, let alone to say how many had entered the work force, how much they earned, what religion they adhered to, whether they were married or single and how many children they had. It is impossible to say at all how many Papuans, not inhabitants of Hanuabada, were working in the town or visiting there.

Hanuabada had long been a meeting place of Papuans and remained so after European contact. Port Moresby, despite its being a white man's town, became another. Octavius Stone[24] described 'Anuapata' in 1875 as 'a regular metropolis and a complete Babel'. More than fifty years later, Jack Hides described Port Moresby as the Rome of Papua. 'There all roads meet . . . From Port Moresby all news and learning are spread wherever police and labourers go.' Of Hanuabada as a meeting place, Hides wrote: 'Mixing continually with the Melanesian villagers of Hanuabada . . . is a polyglot crowd of Papuans.'[25]

The first systematic attempt to count Papuans was made only as a result of the need to tax them. Under the provisions of the Native Taxation Ordinance 1918, as certain areas were declared taxable, a census was taken to discover the number of taxable men in each. In some areas, as in the South Eastern Division, names and money were collected simultaneously.

However inaccurate, these Native Taxation statistics are the only figures that exist. They lump together the twenty-six Motu and Koita villages in the Port Moresby area and for all these give a population of 6416: 1899 adult males, 1677 adult females, 1484 male children under sixteen, and 1359 female children under sixteen. The Motu and Koita villages stretched as far east and as far west as the Port Moresby census district so that these figures may be compared with those for Port Moresby already discussed.

Since 1915, the Resident Magistrate had caused a record of births and deaths to be kept at Hanuabada, Tanobada and Elevala, as part of the government's interest in finding out whether their people were surviving the close contact with Europeans. Since the registration was not compulsory and was carried out by the village constables and since it was in the interest of the government to show an increase of births over deaths, one must treat these figures warily. Births and deaths continued to be counted during the 1920s and 1930s and, together with an estimated total population given every now and then, provide the figures for the Hanuabadan population. In 1926-7 the figure given was 1884.

In the mid-1920s, then, there were about 600 non-Papuan men, women and children inhabiting the Port Moresby census district and about 6500 Papuans. Perhaps 400 non-Papuan men, women and children—mostly white Australians—lived in the township of Port Moresby, next to about 2000 inhabitants of Hanuabada. Nothing discloses those Papuans in Port Moresby who were from other villages in the Central Division, or further afield. There are no figures showing the number of people who worked in Port Moresby, or distinguishing local villagers from migrants. Those who worked as servants to government officials or private residents, as general labourers, tea-makers, gardeners, policemen, messengers, clerks and drivers were not counted. The inhabitants of labour compounds or 'boy houses' did not appear in any census of population until after World War II. They were simply there.

The Papuans who came to Port Moresby understood, or soon learnt, that it was 'the white man's place'.[26] One objection that white men had to natives in towns was that they behaved in a native fashion, and that, unless they were prevented, the residents, being a small minority, would find themselves swamped in a sea of naked or ragged and dirty betel-chewing people who did not use lavatories. Before long residents would be unable to find any part of the town in which they might walk in comfort. 'It is almost impossible for white people to walk along the Beach owing to the cooking, etc. going on among the Hula natives off the canoes', complained Lewis Lett to a Residents' Association meeting which agreed to send a request to the Government Secretary that Ela Beach be kept as a 'reserve for Europeans'.[27] It was a mark of the gulf between Town and Village that this suggestion could have been agreed to, since for generations the Hula people had come to the Motu villages while the men were away on the annual Hiri expedition, the long journey westward to the gulf of Papua when the men of Motu villages carried pots in their large dug-out canoes with the claw-shaped sails, there to exchange them for sago. The Hula people, noted fishermen, kept the old men, the women and children supplied with fish until the return of the expedition when they would be paid in sago or Motu pottery.

Without regulations to control native behaviour, it was agreed, Port Moresby would become another native village; and the existing villages were close enough for white residents to demonstrate that this would mean 'natives making fires, cooking, scratching themselves, and distributing scraps of food, tins and other jetsam,' and producing a 'goodly sample of native smells and quite a few flies, etc.'.[28]

Although some Papuans had to live in the town, conveniently close to the houses of their employers, other native employees were kept outside the town boundaries under the Native Labour Regulations, gazetted in 1914, which specified that Port Moresby employers were required to provide native employees with 'good and sufficient sleeping quarters in a convenient site situated outside the limits of the said Town'.[29] The area around Badili was used for this purpose. Some employees were housed on government property within the boundaries of the town; perhaps to guard the property, perhaps illegally. Close to the European baths, hospital and residents' houses, the 'perpetual jabbering', coughing, barking dogs and howling children of the Papuan employees in the Department of Native Affairs boatshed caused the irritation which moved 'Wide-A-Wake' to write to the paper:

Although we are in a native country, we have not the desire to be amongst native-inhabited buildings along the foreshore or within the town limits, and desire less to be continually annoyed by coloured folk permitted within the town vicinity, unheard of in other native countries.[30]

Well before the arrival of large numbers of white women to the town, well before the fear of the 'Black peril', regulations were made to keep natives out of town as much as possible. The Native Labour Regulations of 1914 forbade a native (other than a domestic servant) 'to enter, remain, or be within or upon' the Town limits of Port Moresby 'after the hour of seven o'clock in the evening' without the written consent of a Magistrate or an Inspector. The Native Regulations of 1908 forbade an employee engaged under the Native Labour Ordinance to be on other premises than those of his employer after 9 p.m. without the written consent of the employer. Employees had to be out of town, or if in the town by necessity, then in their quarters after 9 p.m. The regulations were in part designed to prevent gambling. Seligman, who had visited the town in 1904, had observed that young Motu and Koita servants spend whole nights gambling 'under boatsheds, or other available shelters with the result that they are not fit for work next day.'[31] In 1907, the Native Regulation Ordinance made gambling illegal. Papuans were still gambling enthusiastically and illegally in the 1920s and 1930s.[32] The curfew was marked by the ringing of a bell at 9 p.m. until the power house was built in 1925 when a blast from its whistle was sounded at 8 a.m. and 9 p.m. This was known to Papuans as the 'kibi', the Motu name for a conch shell.[33] The penalty for breach of this Native Regulation was a fine of not more than one month's wages (10/-) or one month's prison.

All natives—not only those covered by the Native Labour Ordinance—were excluded from the town after 9 p.m. by Native Regulation 72(1) which stated that: 'Any native, who, without lawful or reasonable excuse, is found on any premises other than those of his employer (if any) within the township of Port Moresby, between the hours of 9 p.m. and 6 a.m.' was guilty of an offence, for which the penalty was a fine of not more than £1 or imprisonment for not more than two months. 'Premises' under all these regulations included streets, roads, highways, wharves and jetties. The onus of proof of the lawfulness or reasonableness of a native's excuse rested with him, and the plea of being somewhere 'at the invitation of any native male or female' was neither lawful nor reasonable.

The curfew for native labourers was made tighter in November 1925 when its time limit was fixed as 'any time after 9 p.m. and before daylight of the following morning' and not even the written consent of an employer was valid as an excuse for absence from quarters after the hour of 11 p.m.

During those daylight hours when they were allowed in the town, all natives, except small children, had to wear a loin cloth 'or other suitable covering' and behave in a decorous manner. In towns and villages natives had to stop any 'noise, shouting, beating of drums and dancing' at 9 o'clock each night, unless the magistrate's permission had been gained.

The regulation of the native's behaviour towards Europeans applied both in the town and in his village where he was forbidden to use threatening language, to be abusive, insulting or disrespectful to a European, or to beg, either for money or tobacco. How this was to be interpreted was explained later to literate Papuans. 'You must not laugh at a European, or threaten or insult him (that is you must not use "strong talk" to him) . . . When Europeans come into your village you must treat them with respect.'[34] On 19 June 1925, 'X.Y.Z.' claimed space in the *Papuan Courier* to air a matter that he feared might be trivial, but was certainly annoying. 'I refer', he said, 'to the habit of the natives here of walking, lounging and sleeping on, and all over the footpaths . . . Surely it would not be too much to ask that some regulation be passed enforcing natives to keep off the footpaths altogether?' Clearly it was not too much, for on 2 December a regulation was gazetted forbidding any native in Port Moresby to loiter on any footpath 'to the inconvenience of passers by' or from 'wilfully obstructing or impeding the passing of persons along any carriage way or footway.'

Natives and Europeans were kept apart in places of public entertainment, owners of these places having to provide 'separate means of ingress, accommodation and egress' for such under the Public Entertainment Regulations of 1923. Natives (and dogs) were not allowed into the Port Moresby swimming baths under the by-laws of 1923 which were posted up outside the baths. The penalty was a fine not exceeding £5.

Some of the rules keeping European and native apart in Port Moresby were enforced by the police power of the ruling caste, but others were enforced by life itself. The stores had separate serving places for black and white and parts of the store to which natives were not admitted. Both Steamships and Loudon's stores opened soda fountains for the first time in 1926. Steamships set aside a special counter for European customers, where seating was provided and where instead of a glass, patent paper cups were given to each person.[35] Loudon's, who opened theirs later, put it in the chemist's department where 'Europeans only are served'[36] and there is no record of this rule needing to be policed.

Other rules needed the stronger coercive power of the Town Guard, twelve members of the Armed Native Constabulary under the command of the European constable who patrolled the streets of the town, four men on duty during the day and eight at night. In the only year for which this record was published in the *Annual Report*, they carried through 145 successful charges against breaches of the Native Regulations, of which 115 were for gambling, eleven for absence from quarters, sixteen for being unlawfully on premises and three for assault.[37] In the following year, they recorded 291 convictions but the *Annual Report* does not give details.

Films were seen as a source of ideas and a window into a side of European life which might provoke dangerous thoughts. Under the Public Entertainment Regulations of 1923, anyone putting on a display at which natives might be present was required to give a description of each scene to the Government Secretary for his approval, and in 1925 this was amended to apply specifically to films. Each film had first to be shown before a magistrate before it could be shown to an audience which might include a native.

This censorship was the response of the government to a

complaint raised at a meeting of the Chamber of Commerce and Residents' Association. Early in 1925 a motion, moved by R. A. Laws—and passed unanimously—requested closer supervision of films shown to natives. 'In other countries separate nights were kept for natives and they were not allowed to see such films as were shown here' said Laws.[38] 'Coconut' explained to *Bulletin* readers the nature of the danger. Under the heading 'White Sister and Brown Brother' he attacked

> films in which Asiatics or white actors, got up as sheiks or some other branch of nigger, save the white heroine and are affectionately rewarded helps [*sic*] to persuade the coloured spectators, who applaud these dangerous productions heartily, that in real life the colour line is not so rigid as they were led to suppose.[39]

The censorship led to segregated screening in the town later in the year. T. D. Ryan, owner of the picture theatre (and the Top Pub), announced in the *Courier* that whereas in the past he had had to accept only those films which his Sydney agent thought would pass the censorship, he would henceforth import 'first class feature films' and if the censor made any objections, would show them on Wednesdays, 'when only Europeans will be admitted'.[40] He did not have this problem for long: one of the regulations which came out of the panic at the end of the year made it an offence to show *any* film in a place of public entertainment 'at which . . . Europeans and natives are present at the same time.' As so often happened, the government crystallised into law, with penalties, what the residents had informally instituted. From then on there were two screenings. The one advertised in each week's *Courier* was on Saturday night, the films shown were said to be 'the latest' and the *Courier* expected them to attract large European audiences. The charge was three shillings and the patrons sat in deck chairs. The Papuans saw their films early enough to escape the curfew, for the charge of one shilling, and Wild West films were said to be the most popular.

Films were dangerous in another way. The Native Regulations of 1922 prohibited any native—unless with the permission of the Resident Magistrate—from taking part in any scene being photographed 'for the purpose of being . . . reproduced in the moving pictures'. The Lieutenant-Governor, in a memorandum to magistrates for guidance in interpreting this regulation, explained what he had in mind. Permission should be withheld, Murray said, if the scene

   i. suggests anything of a sexual nature
  ii. brings a white woman into close contact with natives though there may be no sexual suggestion
 iii. shows attacks by natives upon Europeans, or by Europeans upon natives, or by natives upon other natives
 iv. shows any criminal action or breach of law whatever, either by natives or others.

Staniforth Smith saw the Papuan as both a child, who must not be shown something for fear that he might try it for himself, and 'like most savage races . . . a sensual man' all of whose passions were excessive. He 'smokes and chews betel nut to excess, and there is no doubt that if he acquired a fondness for drink he would be a slave to the passion'. The Lieutenant-Governor also felt that once a Papuan and a white woman came into close contact even 'though there may be no sexual suggestion' there were dangers in store. This conviction underlies much white thinking in this period.

In 1920 a new misdemeanour was added to the offences of the Criminal Code making it an offence, punishable by one year's imprisonment with hard labour, with or without whipping, to 'enter upon the curtilage of a dwelling house with intent indecently to insult or annoy any female inmate thereof'. Explaining this Ordinance to the Minister for Home and Territories, Judge Herbert (the Acting Administrator) wrote that instances '(all of natives) have occurred where persons (at night time) have entered rooms or verandahs where European women were sleeping. Each time the woman has been awakened by a touch from the intruding native. On none of these occasions had the native (always a servant of the house) any excuse for being where he was.'[41] This amendment, and all other sections of the Criminal

Code, made no distinction as to the colour or 'race' of the female inmate; the tone of Judge Herbert's voice was cool and there had been no public agitation in Port Moresby.

The Australian township of Port Moresby formed 'a thin lid on the kettle' of Papuans,[42] and the white residents sometimes tried to ignore the contents of the kettle, sometimes feared the contents and always tried to ensure that the lid was securely in place.

So oblivious or superior were the residents towards the Papuans that young Harry Rosser went to the Government House children's plain and fancy dress dance as 'KLU [sic] KLUX KLAN'[43] and Mr Dette won the first prize at the Armistice Fancy Dress Ball run by the R.S.S.I.L.A. in 1925 as 'Coon'.[44] Obliviousness became mixed with resentment which grew as the Papuans came to impinge more on the white residents. Some resented money spent on the village and when in 1925 Hanuabada was supplied with street lighting, there was much bitter and inaccurate correspondence in the *Courier* from people who believed that the government was wasting money better spent on lighting Ela Beach Road.[45] In fact, the Hanuabadans had paid for their street lighting themselves, while the government paid for the lighting of the town streets.[46]

Resentment became mixed with fear during the mid-1920s as a new danger was perceived in town life: the danger of sexual overtures by black men to white women. There were dangers here both for Papuans and Europeans. One such danger, seen as such by both, was 'the lady with the towel'. In Vincent Eri's version, the young hero, from an Erema village in the Gulf of Papua, visits his uncle who is a servant in Port Moresby. His uncle's *Sinabada* is in the shower and, having no towel, she calls to the houseboy to bring one. The young man goes with the towel and to his surprise she stands naked before him as he hands her the towel. Confused and disturbed by this revelation, he wonders what she is about, and asks his uncle how he should behave if she were making him an offer. 'If she provokes you, you must never respond', warns his uncle. 'Cooks who think like you end up cooking for other prisoners'.[47] Her actions are never revealed elsewhere so openly in print, though I have heard her story (but never at first hand) from many different sources, including from Stephen Ame of Beipa'a village. She is that newcomer to Papua who does not understand the real nature of the natives. 'Molokihi' (Papua) wrote in the *Bulletin* that the 'Papuan pioneering women, realising the danger, knew how to treat their native servants; the increase in offences of a sexual nature is one of the results of a change in this regard . . . The younger generation of white women . . . overlook that the native is a man.'[48] Such behaviour was also seen to be a danger by the South African Commissioners who had reported: 'This indiscreet conduct on the part of the white woman is said to be more observable in the cases of those who have not grown up in South Africa, and who do not understand the proper manner in which they ought to comport themselves towards the natives.'[49] The danger of sexual relations between black men and white women increasingly preoccupied residents of Port Moresby in the 1920s and 1930s, and Papuans knew of the dangers.

But despite the restrictions and the dangers, Papuans came into Port Moresby to work, to shop, to trade, or to visit friends and relations and see the sights. Many came to earn money to pay their taxes.[50] They must also have been adventurous men, more than usually daring and eager to learn new ways and taste high life. They were at the bottom of the social scale and were the lowest economic group in the town. The usual wage for an indentured labourer in Papua was said to be ten shillings a month all found, though sometimes he earned fifteen. Constables of the Armed Native Constabulary earned ten shillings a month in their first year, rising to twenty in their third; Lance Corporals earned twenty-five shillings a month, Corporals thirty and Sergeants forty. In all these cases, the wages included rations, clothing issue and a blanket. A domestic servant usually earned between ten shillings and £1 a month, but this varied greatly. In 1925, Ellis Silas reported that a 'cook-boy' earned £48 a year. Mekeo cooks from Beipa'a and a Motu domestic servant from Tupuselei insist that they received only five shillings a month in their first year of service.

Native clerks in the government service received ten to twenty shillings a month, rising to £8 in their ninth year of service, though in special cases, the Lieutenant-Governor could agree to engage a clerk at the second, third or even fourth year rates. Clerks received rations and four white sulus (or lap-laps) a year. Clerks in the Government Secretary's department started at ten shillings a month and rose to £7 a month. Papuan staff at the Government Printing Office received the same wages as clerks in the government service. In 1919 the starting wage for a Papuan pastor of the London Missionary Society was £14 a year, and after four years in the job, he reached £16 a year, the maximum stipend for a Papuan pastor. Some with new skills could earn more. The Papuan who ran the refrigeration plant at the wireless station in Port Moresby received £250 a year, Ellis Silas was told. There was a clear caste division in the government wages policy: plantation labourers, police constables, domestic servants, clerks and printing office staff all started on the same salary.

With such salaries, even without the added barriers of caste and colour, there could be very little commerce between Town and Village and none at all between the inhabitants of labour compounds or 'boy houses' and the residents of Port. Even when the residents' ways were adopted by Motuan villagers, interaction was rare. The Hanuabadan cricket club, which for some time had been trying to get a match with the Port Moresby Club, finally succeeded in 1926 as it was found to be impossible to field two white teams. The cricket teams continued separate, playing together only on those rare occasions when the white club could not field two sides. This happened again in 1930 when so many Port residents were away for Easter that the regular match was postponed and a match was arranged between those left in Port and a team of natives from Poreporena. 'Contrary to expectations', reported the *Courier*, 'the boys (the majority of whom were very young) put up a good show.' This was the Moresby of the agitation about sexual assault which flared up in 1925, 1926 and again in 1930. As hostility and fear of an alien group is often expressed in sexual fears and fantasies, apprehension amounting to panic about the possibility of sexual assault on white women by Papuans was not surprising.

The Jews of mediaeval Europe were hated and feared not only because it was believed that they slaughtered Christian children as part of the ritual of making Passover bread (for example the murder of Hugh of Lincoln which is told by Geoffrey Chaucer in the Prioress's Tale), but also because they were seen as satyrs who delighted in polluting Christian girls. This was also an important part of the Nazi case against the Jews. In late nineteenth century Australia, anti-Chinese sentiments were expressed partly as a fear of Chinese ravishing white women. In May 1969, panic swept through the French provincial town of Orleans because it was rumoured that Jewish frock shop proprietors had kidnapped up to twenty-six Christian young women for the white slave traffic, by drugging them in the fitting rooms while they were trying on frocks, and whisking them, through underground passages, to waiting ships (or even submarines) on the nearby River Loire. Yet not one woman had disappeared from the town.[51] As it does not need a disappearing woman in a town to produce an anti-semitic panic, so it does not need a white woman to be raped to produce the constant fear of rape by blacks. It helps to have a white woman touched and it helps immeasurably to have one raped, but it is not necessary. When the White Women's Protection Ordinance was passed in January 1926, no white woman had been raped in Papua.

A small white Australian town with a preponderance of men but which changed during the late 1920s when a large number of white women arrived; a town in which the residents felt more and more fear and dislike of Papuans the more they congregated in the town and the more the natives were influenced by European ways: this was Port Moresby. The colony of which it was capital had a Lieutenant-Governor who was 'essentially a dictator at heart'[52] and who ruled with the advice of official and non-official members, both appointed by himself. Some of the men in the town hated the Lieutenant-Governor and wished him expelled, and many others were discontented with his rule. The 1920s and early 1930s were years of economic depression and the difficulties of the residents were partly blamed on the government. Into this town, a population of Papuans forming a lower social caste than the tiny group of white rulers were coming to work for the white man, to buy in his stores and to learn his ways. In such a town, for a white woman to be peeped at or touched was for white women a frightening experience, for white men, an infamy against white womanhood and an outrage against the prestige of the white race. And in this town it was also a weapon against the policies and personality of the Lieutenant-Governor.

Three   Something very like hysteria

AT dusk on 10 August 1925, a white woman was walking along Port Road, a busy thoroughfare by Port standards. A temporary officer (relieving the Matron of the European hospital, who had been on leave since the end of 1924) she had been posted to Samarai, and was waiting for a ship to take her there. As she walked along the road, she was suddenly attacked by a Papuan. Others walking by ran to the Matron's assistance and frightened off her assailant but not before they identified him. He was arrested the same evening and charged with attempted rape.[1] His attack was to prove the trigger for a new outburst in the township.

The news of the attack spread quickly round the town where many people quickly discovered sexual motives in it. What actually happened to the woman is a mystery. The records of the Central Court in Port Moresby were destroyed in two fires. The court notebooks of Judge Herbert have disappeared; those of Judge Murray are not helpful, being sketchy notes of names, charges and sentences, and those of Judge Gore were lost on a railway station. The newspaper accounts of such cases were intentionally vague. The *Courier* did not often publish the names of women who were attacked and 'made it a practice not to send a representative to report cases of this kind where a white woman has to appear in Court'.[2] The accounts given here and in the next two chapters are therefore very sketchy, depending on findings, sometimes accidental, in other places. The Register of the Central Court exists. This gives the name of the accused, the date on which he was committed for trial, the place, the offence, the names of the judge and prosecutor, the plea and the sentence. An unusually conscientious clerk would make a few notes on each case which might include the name of the plaintiff and some facts of the case. All cases involving European women were marked with the letters E.F. in red ink. Death sentences were also written in red ink.

While the attack was current news, the word got about nine days later that something had happened to the three year old daughter of the Supervisor of Telephones and Mains Engineer. Links were seen between the two occurrences. The editorship of the *Papuan Courier* had been taken over at the end of 1924 by E. A. James, a former public servant, now a private accountant, who continued the role of public agitator which Bruce had begun. His paper discerned a pattern in the attacks and saw them as part of a larger 'problem'. He published an account of the events of the previous two weeks during which, he said, 'three most serious charges' had been laid against natives at the Port Moresby police court and the three committed for trial. These were an attack on 'a white woman on Port Road', an 'assault on a white man occasioning bodily harm' and a 'serious offence' against a 'young female European child'. No names were given in the report. He concluded:

> That the native question was a serious problem has long been recognised, but it is now becoming more, a menace to the Europeans, and particularly to women and children. We may say that the European residents here look expectantly towards the Government to take such steps in the future as are necessary to protect our families from attacks of violence and worse.[3]

The residents' political activities, though circumscribed, were always swift, and during the following week they not only looked expectantly at the Government but acted in the way they had become used to acting when they wanted something done. They agitated. The Chamber of Commerce and Residents' Association, formed as a result of some dissatisfaction with Captain Fitch's handling of the Citizens' Committee, had lost its fire since 1921, and the annual general meeting advertised for 29 July 1925 lapsed for want of a quorum. At the new annual general meeting held on 3 August, those present were the town's businessmen. G. A. Loudon moved that since the 'Residents' had not supported the Association, and only the business people had, the present body should be wound up and a proper Chamber of Commerce formed. A special general meeting was advertised for

The Port Moresby township (Granville West), 1930. Adapted from material supplied by Ian Stuart. Buildings are:

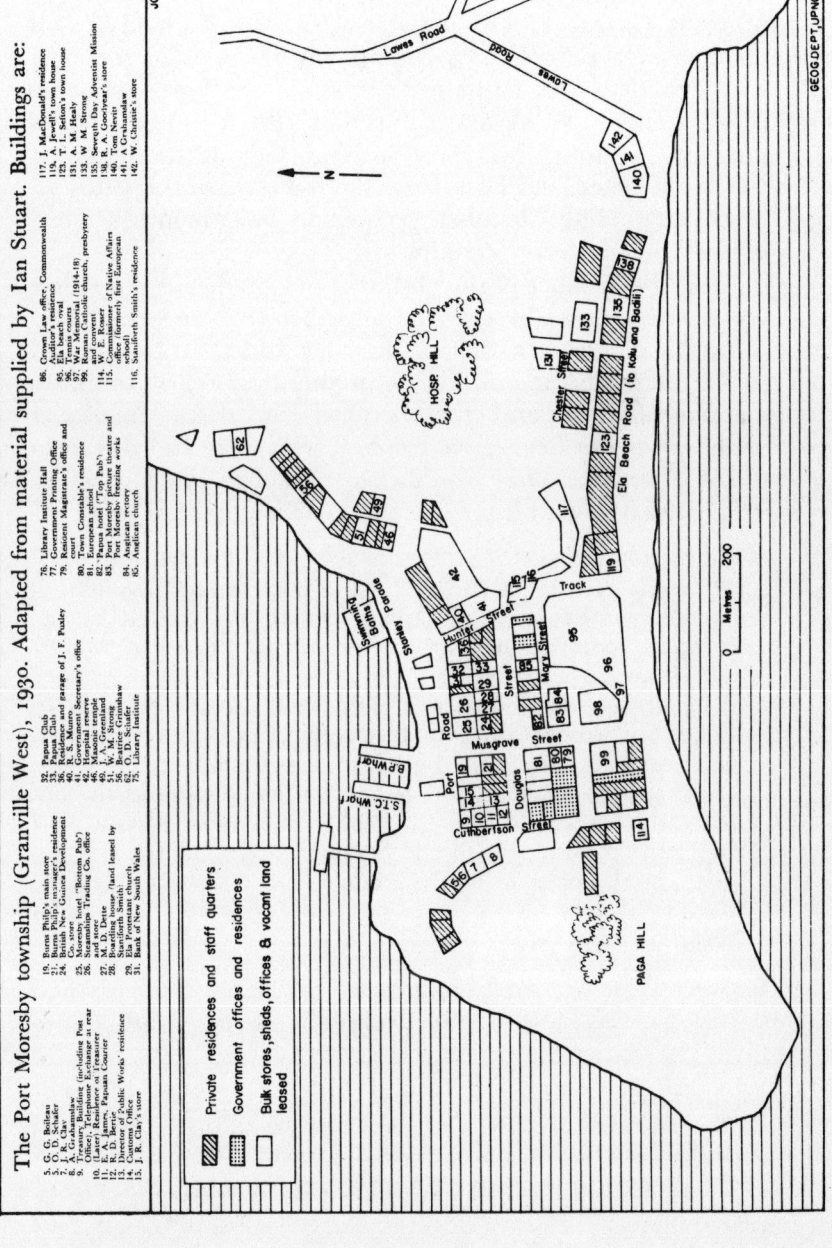

5. G. G. Boileau
6. O. D. Schuler
7. J. K. Clee
8. J. Grahamslaw
9. Treasury Building (including Post Office, Telephone Exchange at rear and store
10. (Later) Residence of Treasurer
11. E. A. James, Papuan Courier
12. R. D. Bertie
13. Director of Public Works' residence
14. Customs Office
15. J. R. Clay's store

19. Burns Philp's main store
21. Burns Philp's manager's residence
24. British New Guinea Development Co. store
25. Moresby hotel (including "Bottom Pub")
26. Steamships Trading Co. office and store
27. M. D. Dute
28. Boarding house—land leased by Staniforth Smith
29. Ela Evangelista church
31. Bank of New South Wales

32. Papua Club
33. Papua Club
38. Residence and garage of J. F. Paxley
40. R. S. Munro
41. Government Secretary's residence
42. Hospital reserve
46. Masonic temple
49. J. L. Greenland
51. W. M. Strong
56. Beatrice Grimshaw
62. O. D. Schuler
75. Library Institute

76. Library Institute Hall
77. Government Printing Office
78. Resident Magistrate's office and court
80. Town Constable's residence
81. European school
82. Papua school ("Top Pub")
83. Port Moresby picture theatre and Port Moresby freezing works
84. Anglican rectory
85. Anglican church

86. Crown Law office, Commonwealth
95. Auditor's residence
96. Ela beach road
97. War Memorial (1914-18)
99. Roman Catholic church, presbytery and convent
114. W. F. Kiser
115. Commissioner of Native Affairs office (formerly first European school)
116. Staniforth Smith's residence

117. J. MacDonald's residence
119. A. Jewell's town house
125. T. Sefton's town house
131. A. M. Healy
133. W. M. Strong
135. Seventh Day Adventist Mission
138. R. A. Goodyear's store
140. Tom Nevin
141. A. Grahamslaw
142. W. Christie's store

Private residences and staff quarters

Government offices and residences

Bulk stores, sheds, offices & vacant land leased

GEOG. DEPT. UPNG

11 August for the purpose of amending the rules and defining the membership of the new Association. The new Port Moresby Chamber of Commerce which was formed at this meeting was the old Association without public servants. The President was Captain A. S. Fitch, the Vice-Presidents G. A. Loudon, R. A. Laws and J. F. Puxley; E. A. James was the Honorary Secretary and the Committee included Sefton, Whitten and Clay from the old days of the Citizens' Association. The Chamber decided to hold monthly meetings as had the former groups.

'At the instance of the Chamber of Commerce' a petition was drawn up on Tuesday, 1 September 1925 and circulated throughout the town during that day and the next. It was to be presented the following night at the first monthly meeting of the Chamber of Commerce to those non-official members of the Legislative Council who were also members of the Chamber. They would then place the petition before the Lieutenant-Governor-in-Council. The petition read:

> We the undersigned Residents of Port Moresby desire to draw the most earnest attention of the Lieutenant-Governor-in-Council to the series of crimes and insults offered to the European population, and particularly to European women and children, by natives.
>
> The effect of the prevalence of these crimes has been to render our womenfolk virtually prisoners in their own homes, which in turn affects the health of the community.
>
> We, your petitioners, feel that in order to suppress the undoubted increase in this class of crime, more drastic and exemplary punishment should be administered by the Government. In the opinion of the Residents, the township of Port Moresby is very inadequately policed, and requires a second European constable.[4]

Between Tuesday and Wednesday 140 adult residents had signed the petition, about two-thirds of the adult white male population of the township.

Two days later, the Hon. J. G. Nelsson, a storekeeper from Woodlark Island, South Eastern Division, who had been in New Guinea since 1881, presented the petition to Murray in the Legislative Council, announcing as he did so that it was 'perfectly respectful in tone' and that it prayed that 'more protection be given to our women and children'. He was perhaps reassuring the Lieutenant-Governor in advance that here was no demand for his removal, nor another telegram to the King. When the petition was read in Council on the following Tuesday, the Lieutenant-Governor replied in terms which showed his displeasure. Angered at the implied criticism of his régime, irritated by the wild exaggeration in the petition, he poured icy judicial water on the fearful residents. He first told them that 'the language used in the petition may have the effect of creating a panic for which there is no justification'. Then, after warning residents that the matter of the Matron was still *sub judice* and ought properly not be discussed at all, proceeded to discuss it, producing facts with which he hoped to cool the residents' overheated fears. The present case, he said, was 'exceptional and unexpected'. So far from being one of a series of a pattern of native assaults, it was 'the only one of its kind' that had taken place for over twenty years and was probably without precedent 'ever since the Central Court was established nearly forty years ago'. To talk of wives being virtual prisoners was 'a dangerous exaggeration' on the part of the petitioners and was 'likely to create a feeling of insecurity which the facts do not warrant'. He expressed shocked surprise at their call for more drastic and exemplary punishment. 'It cannot surely mean', he said, 'that the Government should dictate to a Judge of the Central Court the sentence which he should pass; such action would be quite without precedent in any British community, and would be so obviously unjust that we are sure the petitioners could not contemplate anything of the kind. Yet if the words do not mean this it is difficult to say what they do mean.' He dismissed the request for an extra European constable (on the grounds that in such crimes 'the police can rarely be of any avail in preventing the offence') as he dismissed all their fears. The 'Government cannot see that there is any ground for alarm'.[5]

But a second constable would have made the residents feel more secure and perhaps prevented that feeling of resentment which Murray's judicial dismissal of their fears aroused. It was all very well for Murray to dismiss the attack on the Matron as 'exceptional'; he had no wife or daughter in Port Moresby to be attacked. The tone of the arrogant lawyer could only inflame excited passions but Murray was touchy and defensive. He knew that many white residents believed that his lenient native policy was the cause of these attacks and he rejected this explanation. While in public he discounted their fears in fact he shared the residents' assumptions about native sexuality and its dangers. As an administrator and a defender of a policy he wanted no panic, but at the same time he assumed there was something which the residents would be well advised to be careful of and he expressed his views in despatches to the Minister of State for Home and Territories.

Two days after the Legislative Council meeting Murray sent two despatches to the Minister. The first gave the facts of the three recent cases of assault, much as he had replied to the petitioners but in a far less icy tone of voice. The attack on the Matron, he insisted, was the first case of violent assault upon a white woman and there had never been a case in which the evidence suggested any intention to commit rape, either in his own experience, or in Judge Herbert's or in that of their predecessor, Judge Winter.[6] The attack on the child consisted in their family's fourteen year old houseboy having 'it was said' placed 'his person' against her leg; the third case was one to which he did not think any importance need be attached. It was, incidentally, a case without sexual significance. In the second longer despatch, written after an examination of court records, he included an analysis of those sexual cases which had occurred. 'There have been but few of these attacks and they are not increasing' was the burden of his message. There had been three cases in the previous fifteen years of indecent assault upon small children, all by houseboys. There had been two cases in the last fifteen years of not very serious indecent assault, and in each case both Judges (Murray and Herbert) had suspected that there 'had been previous familiarities between the accused and the girl', and there had been cases of natives found in women's rooms at night but 'the facts all negative any intent to commit rape'.[7]

He was playing down the assaults. A reading of the

court records from 1918 shows that in the seven years 1918-24 there had been three cases of indecent assault upon small children, four cases of indecent assault on women (these may well have been the cases of entering bedrooms) and one case of indecent exposure.[8] But in essence he was right. None of these cases showed any intent to commit rape. This was beside the point for the residents, as the wording of the petition shows. For them *any* manifestations of a sexual nature towards white women or children were either evidence of a desire to rape or, in any case, a sort of symbolic rape. They were evidence of a lack of respect for whites which was dangerous both in itself and because it could lead anywhere. Only with this belief was it conceivable to link together 'crimes and insults' as the petition did. Only in this sort of situation could an insult be as serious as a crime.

Murray noticed in his despatch that the most significant fact about the recent cases was that two of the accused were houseboys and the third was a 'signed-on boy'. This was central to his argument that, in so far as there *was* anything to be fearful of, it was from houseboys or others on indentures, men who had had some contact with European ways. In the light of his facts, it was clear to Murray that the petitioners were both exaggerating the danger and wrongly blaming him. He wrote to the Minister that they were 'giving evidence of something very like hysteria' and said that they had themselves to blame for any attacks which occurred, for in his belief 'a signed-on boy and especially a house-boy is to a great extent what his employer makes him.' Employers in Papua, he said, were on the whole people who did not know how to treat servants, having been in Australia 'men of moderate means who could not afford a servant even if they could find one' and who therefore made particularly bad employers of native servants, alternating between extremes of familiarity and harshness which puzzled natives and were 'not calculated to produce in them that equable courtesy of manner' which we expect from 'inferior races'. While this is important as an indication of how much Murray agreed with the residents' views, and of how a patrician Australian regarded his lower class compatriots, it

65

is by no means a satisfactory explanation for the sexual attacks. Nor is it consistent with his remedies, which included 'the more careful conduct and better influence of the householders and employers themselves' and the end of employing young males as nursemaids for children or in 'close contact with the women of the household'.[9] Here he seemed to agree that native sexuality was such that contact with white women and children was too much for them.

But until it could be proved that the servants who were responsible for sexual advances to women or children were the very ones who worked in those houses where people did not know how to deal with servants or where the women had been lax in their behaviour, the argument was a weak one. Which did not prevent its currency, and the belief that the blame for sexual attacks lay in the behaviour of the women themselves or those in whose households the servants worked was widespread and varied in its expression. In all these explanations there are two strands. One is the anti-female one which blames the women for provoking rape. The other is about the times: they have changed and people no longer filled the same roles as they were wont to do. In the town the master and servant relationship was neither as fixed nor as clearly understood by all sides as it was on the plantation. When everyone knew his role—the villager digging in his village or on the labour line of the plantation, the plantation owner master of his territory and his men—Papua was a more comprehensible and a safer place. The new colonisers were not as clear about their role as the old, and servants became likewise uncertain, which led them to attack white women. In the town, the mythical lady with the towel seemed to typify the wicked temptress who incited chaos.

On the day after the Lieutenant-Governor's reply to the petitioners, the *Courier* published the reply without comment, at the same time reporting the trials of those two Papuans whose actions had been the occasion of the petition. The Matron's attacker, who pleaded not guilty to the charge of attempted rape, was found guilty and sentenced on 10 September 1925 to five years' imprisonment with hard labour under the Criminal Code in which the maximum penalty for his crime was imprisonment with hard labour for fourteen years. The boy who placed 'his person' on the three year old's leg pleaded not guilty to the charge of attempting to have carnal knowledge of a girl under ten—for which the maximum penalty under the Code was imprisonment for life —was found guilty and sentenced on 10 September 1925 to three years' imprisonment with hard labour. These sentences suggest that Judge Herbert at least believed what the offenders to have done to be at the less serious end of those actions which may be termed 'attempted rape' or 'attempted carnal knowledge'. But justice had been brought to bear surely and swiftly—if not to its maximum extent—and both man and boy were punished with prison sentences for their offences only a month after they had committed them. These sentences by no means satisfied the Chamber of Commerce that the government was dealing firmly enough with the problem, nor did they calm the residents' fears. 'A Resident for over 20 years' wrote to the *Courier*:

> I think the whole European community of Papua . . . are agreed that something more than a holiday in Jail is needed as punishment for offences against white women.
>
> The native recently convicted will go to jail and be looked up to with awe and veneration by his fellow prisoners, each one of whom will tell the wonderful story in their villages when their jail period expires and others will desire to emulate their misdeeds.
>
> But how different a public or even jail flogging would make matters; from being a hero, he would be looked on with contempt.
>
> I am not an upholder of flogging, but as an old Resident with a good deal of knowledge of natives & their customs, I consider a flogging—one on sentence and one at expiry—to be the only way to effectively protect our women and children.[10]

And there the matter may have rested, the Lieutenant-Governor pouring scorn on the residents' over-heated imaginations and their overharsh punishments while assuring the Commonwealth Government that the residents had only themselves to blame for attacks. But at the end of the year two more attacks occurred which caused Murray—as a substitute for eating his words and perhaps to forestall another

67

1920 rebellion—to produce a solution both drastic and exemplary. It was a solution to suit all but the most belligerent resident of over twenty years.

The wife of a merchant, a nurse at the European hospital, was asleep there on the night of 24 December 1925 when she was awakened by a man clutching hold of her 'in the fork'. She shouted 'Get out!' and the man ran away, but not before the nurse had recognised him as a fellow hospital employee. He was arrested and admitted that he had done as she said.[11] This information was not published at the time, but was revealed in 1933 when her brother, A. W. Hutchin, M.H.R. for Denison (Tasmania) wrote an angry letter to the Prime Minister complaining about the light sentence given to a Papuan in another case involving this time, the nurse's daughter. Murray sent the Prime Minister the facts of both cases. The second 1925 case was that of a woman living in Petoi in the Gulf Division. She was attacked on 8 December 1925.[12] An odd fact is that the case of a Central Division man found guilty of indecently dealing with an eight year old girl on 26 October 1925 was mentioned neither in the *Papuan Courier* nor in Murray's despatches to the Minister.[13]

On 28 December 1925 Murray sent the following urgent telegram to the Department of Home and Territories.

> Regret report two cases criminal assault white women one Port Moresby one Kerema stop arrests made both cases stop reluctantly forced conclusion much heavier penalties must be provided these offences stop am calling special meeting legislative council to consider bill amending criminal code that respect.[14]

Murray realised that the attacks on the two white women would appear to prove the residents right in their estimation of the dangers and him wrong in his attempts to belittle their fears. The next day his official secretary, Leonard Murray, sent another telegram to the Minister, this time to ask for six copies of a South African report of a Commission appointed to inquire into 'assaults on white women' which had been published in Capetown in 1913.[15] The Commission had actually been appointed to inquire into 'assaults on women' but to Leonard Murray, as to the South African Commissioners, the crucial attacks—and the only ones discussed in the Report—were those on white women.

But Murray believed the matter too urgent to wait the arrival of the report; even before the next ship reached Port he had drawn up a Bill which came before the Executive Council on Wednesday 6 January 1926. R. T. Gore, who had arrived in Papua in 1924 to be Crown Law Officer was official draftsman,[16] but the Bill was very much Murray's.[17] The Executive Council approved the presentation of the Bill to the Legislative Council and a special meeting of that body was called for 8 January to pass it.

'The whole of the European population is behind His Excellency and his Council in this movement', wrote E. A. James. He quoted 'men with considerable experience of the Port Moresby native' to endorse their opinions that the cause of the attacks lay in unmarried natives in town suffering from a repression of sexual instincts, in natives becoming 'flash' and boasting of their conquests with white women, in alcohol, in too mild punishments and in the fact that the natives were 'not sufficiently disciplined'.[18] Government decisions very quickly became public among the tiny white community, for the day on which James wrote these words about a Bill whose provisions he had seen was the day on which it was presented to the Legislative Council.

The men who took their seats in the Legislative Council on Friday 8 January were seven of the official members, three of the four usual non-official members and the new fifth non-official member. The official members were the Director of Agriculture and Commissioner for Lands, Miles Staniforth Smith, the Deputy Chief Judicial Officer, C. E. Herbert, the Government Secretary, H. W. Champion, the Treasurer, R. W. T. Kendrick, the Chief Medical Officer, W. M. Strong, the Commissioner for Native Affairs, L. L. Bell, and the Official Secretary, H. L. Murray. The Director of Public Works, J. T. Bensted, was absent from Papua on leave. The non-official members were J. G. Nelsson, storekeeper from Woodlark Island, A. H. Bunting, a storekeeper from Samarai, and Arthur Jewell, a planter, all three long-time residents of Papua. E. S. Huntley from New Guinea Copper Mines at Tahira, on Bootless Inlet, was absent from

Papua. It was the first Legislative Council meeting for H. M. Dauncey, the oldest white member of the London Missionary Society in Papua, who had been nominated on the recommendation of all the mission bodies to represent their interests. Dauncey sat for only two meetings of the Legislative Council. He resigned because of ill-health in 1928 and his seat was taken by J. B. Clark, another L.M.S. missionary. Dauncey returned to England and died there in 1932. His was the first appointment made since the position had been created by the same amendment to the Papua Act that had provided that a non-official member sit on the Executive Council. The missionaries were keener to be represented than other non-official interests, for no one was elected to fill the Executive Council position until 1932. Dauncey took the oath of allegiance, the oath of office and his seat on the Council just in time to pass the 'White Women's Protection Ordinance', which was the short title that had been given to Sir Hubert Murray's 'Bill for an Act to Amend the Criminal Code'.

The ordinary business of the Papuan Legislative Council was a pretty dull affair, often reading rather as one imagines a session of the Supreme Soviet. Official members outnumbered non-official by two to one, and the non-official members seem to have been chosen neither for their strong 'opposition' viewpoint nor their belligerence in debate. This exchange is fairly typical. It occurred during the 'debate' on the Estimates in 1926, during which non-official members perfunctorily queried most items of expenditure:

Mr Jewell: May I ask why the compassionate allowance
                to Mrs Musgrave has been discontinued?
Mr Champion: She is dead.
Division No. 5 passed as it stands.

On this Friday morning, the debate was more lively. His Excellency was in the chair and after the minutes of the previous meeting had been confirmed and the Admiralty Rules laid on the table and approved, his 'Bill for an Ordinance to Amend the Criminal Code' was introduced: a Bill brief, to the point and extraordinary, both in its harshness and the discrimination of its provisions. It had eight sections.

1. This Ordinance may be cited as the *White Women's Protection Ordinance*, 1926.

2. In this Ordinance unless the context otherwise indicates the terms used respectively shall have the same meanings as are assigned to identical terms by the *Criminal Code*.

3. Any person who commits or attempts to commit the crime of rape upon any European woman or girl shall be guilty of a crime and being convicted thereof shall be liable to the punishment of death.

4. Any person who unlawfully and indecently assaults a European woman or girl shall be guilty of a crime and being convicted thereof shall be liable to imprisonment with or without hard labour for life with or without whipping which may be inflicted once twice or thrice.

5. Any person who—
    (1) has or attempts to have unlawful carnal knowledge of a European girl under the age of fourteen years; or
    (2) unlawfully and indecently deals with a European girl under the age of fourteen years,

shall be guilty of a crime and being convicted thereof shall be liable to imprisonment with or without hard labour for life with or without whipping which may be inflicted once twice or thrice.

6. The punishment of whipping cannot be inflicted upon a person who is sentenced to imprisonment with or without hard labour for a longer term than seven years for any offence under the provisions of this Ordinance.

When an offender is sentenced to whipping the Court is required to give directions in the sentence as to the whipping and may direct that the offender be once twice or thrice privately whipped. The number of strokes which may not exceed fifty at each whipping and in case of an offender under the age of sixteen years may not exceed twenty-five at each whipping and the instrument with which they are to be given must be specified in the sentence.

The instrument must be either a birch rod a leather strap or the instrument commonly called a cat which shall be made of leather or cord without any metallic substance interwoven therewith: Provided that the cat shall not be used in the case of an offender under the age of sixteen years.

The punishment of whipping is not in any case to be inflicted after the expiration of six months from the passing of the sentence.

The punishment of whipping must be inflicted before the offender is put to any employment or labour at any place outside the walls of any prison in which he is confined.

Sections 7 and 8 were technical sections.

The two extraordinary features of the Bill appeared in section 3. First was the distinction as to victim, which had not before been made in the criminal law of any Australian state or in Papua or the Mandated Territory where the law was the Queensland Criminal Code (Adopted). Broadly based on English common law, Australian laws made no distinction in the victims of rape and other sexual assaults between the chaste and the profligate, nor between high and low degree. Even when providing for its colonial children, English law made no caste distinctions; in law, if not in fact, all women were presumed to suffer equally if raped and the penalty for the rapist was identical whether he was black or white. But those who live in a caste society and who administer these laws do make distinctions. The Law Commissioners drafting India's penal code during the years 1834-7 held that a 'chaste high caste female . . . contaminated by the forcible embrace of a man of low caste, or of one who is below caste, say a Chandala or a Pariah' and a woman 'without character or any pretensions to purity, who is wont to be easy of access' might both be victims of a rape, but 'surely the injury is infinitely less in this instance than in the former'.[19] Sir Hubert Murray of Papua, explaining the provisions of his White Women's Protection Ordinance in a despatch to the Australian Government made similar distinctions:

> Doubtless there are native women who set the highest value on their chastity, but they are the exception; and the rape of an ordinary native woman does not present any element of comparison with the rape of a respectable white woman, even where the offence upon the latter is committed by one of her own race and colour.[20]

The assumptions behind this are that respectable women do not enjoy sex, that those who do and are not respectable (like native women) do not care whether they are raped or

72

not. The notion of all sex as rape is there too. Murray's new Ordinance wrote this distinction into the law and provided a new victim, the European woman or girl. Theoretically, the person who commited the crime against her might be of any colour.

The second extraordinary feature of the new law was that it specified that the death penalty, with no alternative, should be provided for rape. Only in two Australian states, New South Wales and Victoria, was death the penalty for rape, and Victoria's law included 'mitigating circumstances' which could prevent the death sentence. Even more extraordinary, the new law provided the death penalty for *attempted* rape. Attempted rape was not even classed as a crime, but a misdemeanour, in all states except Queensland; and in all cases the penalties were limited to fourteen years with hard labour (in Queensland, New South Wales and Western Australia) or not more than seven years (in South Australia) and not more than ten years (in Victoria).

Apart from important changes of principle, the new Bill provided that exemplary punishment which the petitioners of the previous August had prayed for. 'Unlawful and indecent assault' which under the Queensland Criminal Code was defined as a misdemeanour with a punishment of imprisonment with hard labour for two years and under the Native Regulations of imprisonment 'not exceeding six months' was classified under section 4 of the White Women's Protection Ordinance as a crime for which the penalty was imprisonment with or without hard labour for life with or without one, two or three whippings. The new law raised the age of white girls of whom it was unlawful to have carnal knowledge from the twelve years of the Criminal Code to fourteen years. It enabled the judge to order more whippings —the maximum number under the Code was two—and it added whipping to more punishments. Under the Code it was not possible to order whipping to any sentence of more than two years' imprisonment, now a judge could order a whipping to be added to any sentence of up to seven years.

Before the Bill was read the first time, Murray made a statement. The Bill, he said, represented his own views, but he had no desire to force these views on members and he welcomed discussion. He made no mention of the petition, ate none of his icy words of August nor any humble pie, simply drew attention to two matters which must have caused division on the Executive Council but without mentioning any disagreement. 'It will be seen', he said, 'that rape and attempted rape are both made capital offences but that the Bill contains no new provisions as to flogging.' Since the Bill *did* contain new provisions as to flogging, he must have been referring to the question of public flogging raised by 'Resident of over 20 years' and supported by some members of the Legislative Council. He did not believe that private flogging would be a deterrent, or that public flogging would be tolerated, and nothing short of death would be a 'sufficient and immediate deterrent to the commission of the crimes mentioned'.

The Government Secretary put the official case for the Bill. He read figures to show that 'these offences' had increased: from 1904 to 1913 there had been not a single conviction recorded; from 1914 to 1918 there had been two; from 1919 to 1921 three; and from 1922 to 1925 'not only were the cases more serious but there were no less than eight convictions, with two more cases pending'.[21] This is what the white residents had been contending since August. This is what Murray had denied firmly to the Commonwealth Government in September when he said that the attacks were few and not increasing. Only the cases of the two women had taken place since.[22] That the White Women's Protection Ordinance was in detail Murray's Bill became clear when two official members—one of whom was Judge Herbert—joined the non-official members in expressing disapproval of important parts of it. Although standing orders had been suspended to enable the Bill to go through all its stages in a day, the Council adjourned on the motion of Nelsson and Jewell, but only until the next day, Saturday, the first Saturday on which it had met for six years. On the question of principle—that it was a different and more serious crime to rape or attempt to rape a white woman than a black one—as on the present need for white women to be protected, all members absolutely agreed.

When the Council met again on Saturday morning,

Jewell made the first attempt to change the Bill. He moved that in clause 3 the words 'or attempt to commit' be deleted and his motion was seconded by the Chief Medical Officer. Their reason was simply that it was unjust to punish the attempt to rape as severely as the act of rape, particularly if the only punishment for the act were to be the ultimate one of death. Judge Herbert had already given the legal argument against this provision: that there was no precedent for punishing an attempt as severely as the commission of a crime. Those who agreed with Hubert Murray must have already counted heads and as they had no electorate and no need to debate, they quietly voted against the amendment and defeated it by six votes to five. It was an interesting division since two senior official members voted against the government together with three non-official members, while one non-official member joined the government side. J. T. Bensted wrote years later that, had he been there, he would have voted against the government which would have produced a deadlock and forced the Lieutenant-Governor to use his own vote.[23]

On the complicated and emotional issue of flogging, there was far less opposition. Dr Strong's attempt to reduce the penalty had much less chance of success than Jewell's, for it existed already under the Criminal Code. Strong moved that the whipping provisions of the Bill be amended so that the words 'twice or thrice' be omitted. 'I doubt,' he said, 'if three floggings of fifty strokes with a cat would occur at the present time in any civilized country, and if it did I think there would be an immediate outcry against it and that steps would be taken to see that the same did not occur again.' Staniforth Smith, Murray's old enemy, eloquently expressed the views of the majority of the Council:

May I emphasize the fact that, so far as this Bill is concerned, this is not a civilized country. We are dealing with a primitive native race . . . We are dealing with a native race which is emerging from a state of barbarism, and in all these races passions are strong and liable to lead to the most awful results . . . None of us like the idea of flogging, and none of us like the idea of capital punishment, but we are all agreed that even capital punishment, or even the horror of flogging

75

with the cat, is preferable to the greater horror of white women and young children being violated by natives. This had not happened so far, but there have been attempts . . .

Only his seconder, Dauncey, and A. H. Bunting voted with Dr Strong, whose amendment was lost by eight votes to three. Defeated in his attempt, the Chief Medical Officer—who was also Government Anthropologist—then tried to convince the Council that if flogging were to be a deterrent and not simply a punishment, it had to be public. Here opinion divided more evenly. Dauncey agreed that flogging should be public. Flogging was 'brutal perhaps', he said, 'but we are dealing with a very serious matter. The surgeon's knife is brutal but it has to be used.' Staniforth Smith again presented the government position, this time against public flogging, and he used a favourite argument of Papuan colonial administrators. 'Do you think', he asked, 'that the Australian people of the present time would like to see photographs of public floggings of natives in Papua?' Some would not have liked it at all, but whether that would have prevented it from happening was another matter. Staniforth Smith voiced the general assumption that the Bill was meant only to apply to 'natives'. Jewell, arguing for public flogging, reminded members that the Bill applied to 'both Europeans and natives alike', but in fact no one expected that the provisions of the Ordinance would ever be applied to a white man. Strong's motion was lost. All the non-official members voted with him and the official members against him. They must all have known that it would have been difficult to have public flogging accepted by the Australian government. Strong must have known it too. His speeches on public flogging seem inconsistent. Why should a humane man who believed that three floggings were barbarous support the barbarity of public punishment? He probably believed, having lost the day on the reduction of the number of floggings, that if he lured his opponents into supporting public flogging— the consistent position if they saw flogging as a deterrent, not simply revenge—Australian reaction to this would cause its total abolition. His ironic speech on public punishment epitomised the colonial paradox:

I certainly had begun to consider Papua as a civilized country. When it was an uncivilized country these punishments were not needed. It is agreed on all sides that serious offences of this kind are a recent thing, and I would be quite loath indeed to believe that the civilization we have introduced has resulted in the country becoming so uncivilized that we have to inflict punishment that we would not have done when it was not at all civilized.

Strong made yet another attempt to reduce flogging, moving that the number of strokes permissible each time be reduced from fifty to twenty-five, but he was again defeated: only Dauncey and Bunting voted with him.

Though he was the author of this unreasonable Bill, Murray could not resist giving the members of the Council a lesson in reason and the judicial examination of facts. He did not seriously intervene in the debate, but asked questions here and there. His longest intervention came towards the end, in reply to Dauncey. Dauncey was convinced that it was 'the ne'er do wells of half Papua'[24] meeting in Port Moresby while looking for jobs or just hanging about Koke, who were the attackers of white women and children. They ought to be sent back to their villages, he said, voicing the puritan conviction about the devil and idle hands, the parental conviction about unsupervised children, and the colonial conviction that a group of natives is a mob. His Excellency gave Dauncey a cool reply. 'It is not these boys who commit these sexual offences. The last three cases were signed-on boys.'[25] But as Murray's facts would have created too many new problems to deal with then, and as it seemed perfectly obvious that men wandering around a town were up to no good, Dauncey's beliefs prevailed and Murray soon gave them legislative form.

The Legislative Council in committee agreed to all the clauses of the Bill as they stood and passed two small drafting amendments moved by Judge Herbert and supported by the government. So the Bill passed all its stages, the Committee turned itself back into a Council, received its own report that it had passed the Bill, and heard it read a third time. On the motion of the Government Secretary, with the Treasurer seconding, that 'the Bill do now pass' it was passed with no dissenting voice. The clerk presented the Bill to His Excellency for his assent thereto, and on this being given, the Council adjourned *sine die*.

A few days after the Ordinance had been agreed to, Murray sent three copies of it to the Minister together with a long despatch explaining its provisions, explanations he had not vouchsafed to the members of the Legislative Council. It was 'unfortunately considered necessary to provide the death penalty for the attempt, and as the law recognises no higher penalty, we must punish the completed crime with death also. I regret to say that I consider this very drastic punishment to be necessary and indeed *it was at my suggestion that it was included in this Bill.*' (my italics). Why then had Murray not explained this when Jewell and his four supporters had tried to reduce the penalty for attempted rape? Had Murray not confided his views to his Executive Council, some of whom voted with Jewell? Or was the vote for Jewell's amendment by the official members in fact a vote against capital punishment? It is clear from Murray's despatch to the Minister that he intended to use the death penalty to punish and deter acts which might be called attempted rape and the Ordinance was in fact more drastic in intent than it appeared.

In explaining to the Minister the distinction as to victim, Murray put the view of the white residents that it was 'reasonable', since the rape of an 'ordinary native woman' did not present 'any element of comparison' with that of a 'respectable white woman'. But despite his agreement and despite the Ordinance, he could not agree that 'this revolting form of sex problem' would be prevented by these means.[26] Murray was caught between the pressure of the white residents who blamed his policy for the attacks, his own belief about the cause of the attacks, and his assessment of the reaction of the Australian Government. Clearly uneasy about some aspects of his White Women's Protection Ordinance, his account of it in the *Annual Report* for 1925-6, written in his clearest prose, is belligerent and dishonest. He insisted first that the penalties for rape and attempted rape applied to all such crimes committed 'whether by a native or by anyone else' which was in theory true but less than honest

78

since, though the Ordinance did not say 'any native' but 'any person' the whole history of its existence demonstrated its intention and how it would be applied. Murray then gave an account of the new distinction in the victim of the outrage and in the penalty exacted for rape, attempted rape and indecent assault against a white woman and a Papuan woman. He defended both. 'There had, so far as I am aware, never been a case of the rape of a native woman by a white man in Papua, and only two cases of attempted rape, both of which (tried of course without jury) resulted in an acquittal.' He was less than honest here. In the first place, he failed to say that neither had there been a case of rape of a white woman by a Papuan, but the Ordinance had seemed necessary despite this. In the second place, the fact that the white men had been acquitted of attempted rape meant little; it would have been almost impossible for a Papuan to win a case against a white man in Port Moresby. 'It is, in fact', he had himself written in 1922, 'quite impossible to administer even handed justice in these countries—public opinion is so strong against it and one has to be so certain that one is right; and a native must have a very strong case indeed to get a conviction against a white man.'[27]

Finally, and most significantly, on the absence of rape by white men he was wilfully misleading. Even if he had forgotten the cases of the Resident Magistrate and the Boundary Commission official in 1912,[28] he could scarcely have forgotten his own despatch of November 1925, only seven months before, when he reported to the Minister that during a recent tour of inspection to Samarai with members of the Executive Council, he had received information justifying proceedings against two Europeans, one for sodomy with a native boy, the other for rape against a native woman. Yet there had been no trial. The members of the Executive Council had argued that, in the sodomy case, the man should not be prosecuted provided he gave an undertaking to leave the country, an argument based on compassion for his respected wife and her children. The Lieutenant-Governor agreed in this case, but was reluctant in the rape case where he felt no such grounds for leniency existed and where leniency might be dangerous. 'It would be disastrous to the prestige of the white man', he had written to the Minister, 'if the natives imagined that we regarded such atrocities with indifference and that such crimes could be committed by white men without fear of punishment, but I do not think they will look on our action in this way'.[29] It is difficult to see why he thought this, and he did not explain. In the event he agreed with the other members of the Executive that having done it for one they ought to do it for the other; both men left the Territory without being prosecuted and the cases never were made public. Here again he had agreed in essence with the white residents in seeing not justice nor humanity at stake but 'white prestige' and expediency.

Murray wrote to his sister-in-law Lady Mary Murray a few months after the passage of the Ordinance. 'We had an epidemic of assaults by natives on white women last year. Of course our native policy was blamed at first—we spoil the natives and so forth—but the real reason was the carelessness of the white women themselves, who do not seem to realise that a native is a man with a man's passions, and commonly very little self-control. Everybody has now come round to this view—including even the white women.'[30] He had never publicly admitted in Papua that there had been an 'epidemic' of assaults and to say that 'everyone including even the white women' had come round to his own view was to show the autocrat's tendency to confuse the wish with the fact.

After the Ordinance had been passed, it still had to gain the Australian Government's approval before it could become law. Correspondents from Papua writing to the Sydney *Bulletin* gave Australian readers their own explanation of those sexual attacks which had made the Ordinance a necessity. It was the missions, wrote 'Bouragi' which, by abolishing that sexual freedom which traditionally young Papuans had enjoyed, had left them frustrated and constantly in need of sexual gratification. 'Molokihi' did not entirely agree, blaming rather the 'younger generation of white women' who did not understand how natives should be treated. 'Gregor' also blamed the missions for their opposition to the employment of native women for domestic work,[31] and the government for succumbing to mission pressure and passing a 'ridiculous regulation' to this effect.[32]

'Coconut' blamed white women, especially those depraved ones, 'own sisters to the film-doped and jazz-crazed young loafers to be encountered in Melbourne and Sydney, who take a pride in announcing that they are "shot"—who make advances to the coloured boys'.[33] Something similar was believed in 1913 by the South African Commissioners, where the culprits were 'foreign prostitutes' and by the Administration employee travelling south in 1971 who knew the culprits to be 'female hippies'.[34] Mrs F. L. Clarke, the wife of a 'rubber and coconut plantation owner' on her annual holidays in Melbourne, told readers of the Melbourne *Herald* from her headquarters in Scott's Hotel, about the atmosphere in Port Moresby and the necessity for the Ordinance. 'Women dare not go out alone. If they do they carry revolvers', she said, and opined that public flogging was 'the only way to deal with natives.'[35]

But these explanations did not satisfy Australian public opinion altogether and there was uneasiness. The Minister for Home and Territories, Senator G. F. Pearce, expressed his government's uneasiness in his answer to a question in the House of Representatives from Dr William Maloney (Melbourne) who asked whether the Ordinance had been submitted to the Commonwealth Government for its assent, and whether the House would have an opportunity to debate 'the proposed serious series of punishments for the natives of Papua.'[36] The Minister's specious reply merely explained that press reports which described the Ordinance as applying only to native offenders were inaccurate. He said that the relevant sections of the Act applied 'to white men equally with natives' and hoped that would satisfy questioners. But as more newspaper accounts appeared and Senator Pearce's answer to Dr Maloney was reported, there was more uneasiness. A Mrs Effie Sandery described as an 'authoress' and 'the first white woman to enter the cannibal village of Baramura alone',[37] thought too much publicity was being given to 'the very rare cases of attack'.[38] John Kent, described as a missionary for twenty years in Papua, when asked to comment on the Ordinance expressed surprise that 'such drastic measures had been found necessary to cope with the assaults by natives on white women, which were to his knowledge few and far between'.[39]

Discussion in the Australian press and Parliament coincided with the Commonwealth Government's decision on the ordinance. On 10 February it was sent to the Attorney-General's department for approval with a note from the Home and Territories department about Dr Maloney's question in the House of Representatives. In the minute paper prepared for the Attorney-General, R. R. Garran, the Solicitor-General, clearly set out the views of the Lieutenant-Governor of Papua and stated of the Ordinance that it 'is aimed at native offenders'.[40] The Attorney-General, still uneasy about the death penalty for *attempted* rape, asked for a discussion with Murray who was due in Australia shortly. After these discussions he wrote the following note:

> The Lieutenant-Governor assures me that the native mind cannot distinguish between 'an attempt' and the 'act' itself and that, in order to make the legislation effective, the attempt must be punished in the same way as the act. The ordinance has been widely proclaimed. I am not prepared to recommend over ruling the deliberate judgement, in an important and difficult matter, of a local authority.[41]

He approved the Ordinance, the Governor-General signed, the approval was published in the *Commonwealth Gazette* and some days later telegraphed to Port Moresby.

When the Lieutenant-Governor arrived in Melbourne in March, a reporter interviewing him for the Melbourne *Herald* asked about the White Women's Protection Ordinance. 'There must be different punishments for blacks and whites' he was reported to have said, thus contradicting the Minister's explanation. Yet when the Ordinance was tabled in the House of Representatives in May of 1926, no voice was raised against it.

Two days after the Ordinance had passed through the Papuan Legislative Council, a Papuan appeared in the Port Moresby Central Court before Mr Justice Herbert charged with attempted rape, with indecent assault and with assault occasioning bodily harm. He was the nurse's night time assailant. He was found guilty of indecent assault and received the maximum penalty under the Criminal Code of two years' imprisonment with hard labour and a whipping.

As the Judge sentenced him reluctantly to a whipping for what he had done at the hospital where these women were doing good to the sick, he spoke to the accused through an interpreter:

Tell the accused I find him guilty of indecent assault. He is a very lucky boy. If he had done that thing now, he might go to gaol for life. He can tell every boy that anyone who treats sinabadas like he had done can now be given gaol for life . . . I hope this punishment with the new law will stop boys from doing these things. Two years' imprisonment is all I can give him: if I could give him more, I would.[42]

The government did not rely on admonishment alone. If the Ordinance was to have any effect as a deterrent, Papuans would have to know of its existence and of the harshness of its provisions. Hence a copy was sent to each Magistrate with a covering letter directing that officers make the provisions of the Ordinance known to all natives of their Division or District. 'It is not of course to be expected', the letter explained, 'that natives can grasp the distinction between the various offences mentioned in the Ordinance, but they should clearly understand that any interference whatever with a white woman or girl will in future be dealt with much more severely than in the past, and will be punished with death or with a long term of imprisonment or a flogging.'[43] The government also sent out a copy of the effects of the Ordinance printed in local languages; a copy in the Mekeo language is printed here. How it was understood by some Papuans is recalled by Stephen Ame from Beipa'a: 'If a Papuan smiled at a white woman,' he says, 'he was gaoled; if he looked at her, he was gaoled; if he touched her, he was gaoled; if he touched her on the breast, he would be hanged.'[44]

After the Ordinance had become law, the government supported its harsh penalties by stopping up existing gaps through which Papuans could get into towns and come in contact with white women, and by building up more walls to keep apart those who were already in the towns. Dauncey's fears about the 'ne'er do wells' were answered within two months, despite Murray's arguments, by a new Regulation dealing with 'foreign natives', which meant any native 'absent from his tribal village' except indentured labour, government or mission employees. Such foreign natives who could not give a magistrate a good enough account of their means of support could now be ordered out of the towns of Port Moresby and Samarai and back to their village or district. The ·penalty for disobeying this regulation was imprisonment for up to six months. Any native convicted and sentenced to a prison term under the White Women's Protection Ordinance was specially provided for under a new regulation stating that after the expiry of his prison term he must not 'come or remain within the boundaries of any town in the Territory'. The penalty was imprisonment for up to six months. To ensure that men convicted of offences against white women were not employed, a blacklist was drawn up by the Department of Native Affairs containing the names of Papuans who were not to be 'signed-on'. The list was kept in the Labour Office and referred to when contracts of service were being drawn up.[45] The Department of Native Affairs sent circular letters to out-stations giving information about Papuans with such convictions and adding that the magistrate should in future not consent to the engagement of these natives under contract of service.[46] These regulations covered indentured labourers, but when free labour—under certain circumstances—was allowed in the following year a problem was created. When the Natives (Non-Indentured service) Ordinance 1927 was being debated in the Legislative Council, Dauncey wondered what its effect would be on those on the Department of Native Affairs blacklist who were not allowed to be signed on and whether this new ordinance might mean that they would be able to engage as free labour. His concern met no response. By March 1930 there were twenty-five names on the blacklist.[47]

Another separating wall was built by a new set of regulations, passed in March of 1926 making it an offence to present 'any cinematograph exhibition' in 'any place of public entertainment at which exhibitions Europeans and natives are present at the same time'. Moving pictures, featuring as they often did violence and sexual passion, had earlier been supposed a source of danger but now a connection was assumed between viewing films and attacking white women.

On 8 March 1926 the Intermission Conference, meeting at Kwato, discussed the White Women's Protection Ordinance, among other items. Representatives of the Anglican mission, the L.M.S., the Kwato Extension Service and the Methodist Missionary Society unanimously agreed to a resolution moved by the Bishop of New Guinea and seconded by H. M. Dauncey. The conference expressed its 'thankfulness for the recent ordinance for the protection of white women' and respectfully asked the government to 'make the punishment for offences against Papuan women more severe, and to instruct the magistrates to take a more serious view of adultery in the case of Papuans and of neglect of married men to support their children in the case of desertion'. The conference felt strongly that such action would have good effect in 'showing that the Government is concerned with respect due to women, Papuan as well as white'.[48]

It was, even as a gesture, pretty ineffectual in the face of the Ordinance and the structure of regulations built around it. But it was a gesture. There was no publicity given to this resolution and it was not put into effect by the government.

The savagery of the Ordinance, with its discriminatory provisions and the fact that it was passed not five months after Murray's rejection of the residents' petition, are strange and murky aspects of Murray's beliefs and his native policy which obviously call for some explanation, though none has been given by Murray's biographers.

This is the account given by Lewis Lett of the events of 1925 and 1926. I give it in full, since his account is wrong in almost every detail:

There had been a number of cases of assault on white women by native servants and others; some serious, others quite trivial. Public opinion, spurred on by feminine resentment, rose to a high pitch. The white women of Port Moresby, many of them quite new to tropical conditions, did not seem to understand that the native servants are human . . . They were, many of them, inclined to be careless about their dress and unduly familiar with their native servants—far more careless than they would think of being with men of their own colour, and the natives reacted as might be expected from people barely removed from savagery. The men of the town were spurred by their women to protest, and their protest took the form of accusing the Government of lethargy in the matter. The laws, they said, were not sufficiently severe, and did not provide heavy enough penalties for such offences as were complained of.

The situation was peculiar. The government knew, the protesting men knew, and the white women knew, that the cause of the phase was carelessness on the part of the women. But none of the three would openly declare the truth; the Government from scruples due to tact, the men because they were driven by a desire to protect their women both from native offenders and from the accusation of remissness, and the women themselves by the age-old reluctance to admit themselves in the wrong. A deputation of the townspeople was received by the Lieutenant-Governor in the presence of the Legislative Council. The Lieutenant-Governor was quite obviously bored by the recommendation of measures which had been considered and rejected long ago by him and his Council, and was stung to cold anger by the proposal that flogging should be made a penalty for offences under the new Act. He readily agreed to a dozen petty and quite useless precautions that the deputation recommended, and dismissed its members with the feeling that they had wasted their time and made themselves more than a little ridiculous.

The new Act authorized the death penalty for extreme offences; but the sudden and complete cessation of the series of assaults was due, not to any new precautions, but to the action of the Government in spreading assiduously among the natives the news of the passage of the Protection Act with its death penalty, and the warning that its provisions would be exercised fully in the case of future offenders.[49]

Lett's admiration for Sir Hubert Murray confused his judgment as it may have blurred his memory. There was no deputation in 1925 or 1926. Lett telescoped two events, the petition of 1925 which preceded the passage of the Ordinance and a deputation—of which he was himself a member—in 1930. If Murray agreed, as Lett asserts, to 'a dozen petty and useless precautions' they did not appear in the Ordinance which was clear and concise about serious crimes and large penalties. Flogging *was* a penalty under the new Ordinance, as it was already under the Criminal Code; there was now more of it. And most important of all, there was no 'sudden

TRANSLATION

OF THE EFFECT OF THE

White Women's Protection Ordinance, 1926

IN THE DIALECT OF MEKEO.

Kabana alapu mamanga e kapaia New Guinea au angao nao papiei, nao iviaoi e lapau pengii : e palifui koa, ava aungo'i ane pengia.

Kaimo kaimo ina alapu laangai ane aopangai, inipo mao kipulai ane angue ke kipulai e angu laolao faokiai ingapuka oio ake pa mia, kina angaongai ouanga ima, kina angaongai ouanga ima, kina angaongai ouanga ima.

Kabana aunga e iva koa, ngaina lifu aunga kipulai ane pa koko umajia, kipulai ane mae, aiio ma ane laa Kabana ifo.

Kabana ngaina alapu mamanga e ongeia, New Guinea au apala'i ia'i nao papiei, nao iviaoi feke afiapalangii koa ava aungo'i kenga afia e oma.

Port Moresby :
EDWARD GEORGE BAKER, Government Printer.—3965/3.26.—200.

Ordinance kindly lent by Fr Diaz, Roman Catholic Mission, Beipa'a. As translated by Martha Ila of Boroko, it reads :

1. The Government has made a new law which says that any New Guinean man who makes advances to a white woman or girl and causes her harm will be punished severely.

2. Anyone who disobeys this law will be sent to prison and will also be beaten with a cane fifty times a day for three days.

3. The Government has also said that the wrongdoer will be put in prison for life and, if the Government wishes, he will be hanged.

4. The Government has made this new law so that New Guinean men who cause harm to white women or girls will be punished.

Port Moresby, about 1938. The photo, taken from an aerial survey plane, is reproduced by permission from the New Guinea Collection of the University of Papua New Guinea Library.

Port Moresby wharf, from an album of photos taken by Colonel Lovett Cameron, Djaul Plantation, New Ireland. Reproduced by permission from the New Guinea Collection, University of Papua New Guinea Library.

The Legislative Council, 1931, reproduced by permission from *Papuan Villager*, Vol. 3, no. 9, 15 September 1931, p. 69.

Back row L. to R.: Hon. C. R. Pinney (Commissioner for Lands), Hon. H. L. Murray (Official Secretary), Hon. E. C. Harris (Treasurer), Hon. W. M. Strong (Chief Medical Officer), Hon. H. W. Champion (Government Secretary), Hon. A. P. Lyons (Director of Public Works), Hon. J. T. O'Malley (Commissioner for Native Affairs).

Front row L. to R.: Hon. G. W. Guttridge (Non-official member), Hon. J. G. Nelsson (Non-official member), His Excellency Sir Hubert Murray, K.C.M.G. (Lieutenant-Governor), Hon. A. Jewell (Non-official member).

and complete cessation of the series of assaults' unless the series is defined as those assaults which occurred before the passage of the Ordinance.

Lett's determination to give Murray all the credit for everything good which was done by the Papuan administration, but none of the blame for that which was not good, lands him into some difficulties. If Murray thought the residents so wrong-headed, why then did he bow to the demands of their ignorant or even wicked wives? If the attacks were not serious and the women themselves to blame for inciting both the attacks and their husbands' agitation, then surely an enlightened governor might have organised a series of lectures to the women (by One-Who-Knew-Better?) on how to deal with native servants, how to dress, speak and behave and how always to check that there was a towel in the bathroom.

Lett, following Murray, laid all the blame on the women. The symbolic lady with the towel or the flimsy nightgown is cast by him in the new and more militant role of the nagging wife urging a reluctant husband to petition and protest and change laws to protect her against imaginary attacks. He assembles no evidence for his assertion that the women spurred the men to protest, nor for his other that their husbands knew the women were themselves to blame. Everything that we have seen about Port Moresby society at at this time argues against such an assertion.

J. T. Bensted, in a long review of Lett's book, took issue with this explanation of the events. Bensted admired Murray, but less idolatrously than Lett. He was a member of the Executive Council and worked closely with the Lieutenant-Governor for many years. To Bensted, the 'passing of the Ordinance was a case of the "expediency" which Mr Lett claims was never practised by Sir Hubert. There was no necessity for the passing of any such drastic law, and Sir Hubert knew it, but bowed to public clamour.'[50] H. W. Champion, Government Secretary throughout these years, believed the same in 1970.[51] Francis West, Murray's most recent biographer, not only essays no explanation of the White Women's Protection Ordinance, he never even mentions it.

Bensted, Champion and Lett all agree that public presure was strong. And clearly it was. Murray had succumbed to the residents' pressure in the hope that they would be satisfied. Lett wrote in his book that in succumbing, he successfully put an end to the attacks. Both the hope and the account were false.

Four Miaro

THOUGH the noose of the Ordinance hung over every Papuan and though the white residents hoped that it would restrain them, the cases of assault brought before the Central Court did not cease. Papuans in Port Moresby continued at the least to be curious enough about white women to risk heavy penalties for looking at them or touching them and, at the most, foolhardy enough or resentful enough or aggressive enough to risk death for trying to lie with them.

According to the Register of Criminal Cases of the Central Court there were more such cases, not fewer, after the passage of the White Women's Protection Ordinance. H. W. Champion had told the Legislative Council of thirteen cases involving white women in the twelve years before the passage of the Ordinance and two which were pending while the Ordinance was being passed. In the two years to the end of 1928, eight Papuans accused of assaults against white women appeared before the Central Court and all but one were convicted. The first such case to come before the Central Court after the Ordinance was in August 1926; it was a case of indecent assault of a European female. Whatever the reason one might give for the attacks, the fact was that there was no 'sudden and complete cessation' of them.[1]

The attacks varied in seriousness from that of the man, who in August 1927, was charged with being in a dwelling with intent indecently to annoy a female inmate, for which he received three months' imprisonment with hard labour, to another, charged with unlawfully and indecently dealing with a European girl under fourteen, who was sentenced to imprisonment for life with hard labour. There were many 'curtilage' cases, where Papuans were found within the boundaries of a dwelling and arrested. They had not performed an assault, but were unlawfully on premises and assumed to be there with intent indecently to annoy a female inmate.[2] One such case tried before Judge Murray in June

1930 involved the wife of the Central Court Judge, who was standing in her night attire on the verandah of her house on Paga Hill when she heard a noise in the garden. Shining her torch on to the garden, she lit up a Papuan who ran away. Later a suspect was brought along and recognised. He was arrested and charged under section 420A of the Criminal Code. In the Central Court the accused, a house servant employed by G. M. Turnbull, the Public Works Department architect, gave evidence that he had gone to the Judge's house to borrow tobacco from the servant and had overstayed the 9.00 p.m. whistle. His evidence was supported by the servant. When Judge Murray requested evidence of the accused's intent to do harm, the Crown Prosecutor said: 'the boy was on a side of the house where he had no reasonable excuse for being, it was a place where he would not naturally be'.[3] Judge Murray considered this inadequate evidence of intent, found the accused not guilty and discharged him. It was a rare verdict: he was one of only four men charged with such offences against white women to be discharged up to the period of World War II.

The most common form of assault upon white women, and the one which the Ordinance had been specifically designed to stamp out, was of the kind that came before the Central Court on 16 September 1927. Late at night a Papuan entered a bedroom and, lifting the bedclothes, had put his hand on the bare thigh of a sleeping woman. She was 'awakened by this act and endeavoured to hold the accused but he succeeded in making his escape'.[4] He was later arrested on the evidence of his fellow employees, to whom he was said to have confided his exploits, and charged under section 4 of the White Women's Protection Ordinance with unlawfully and indecently assaulting a European woman, for which the maximum penalty was imprisonment with hard labour for life, with or without a whipping. Found guilty, he was sentenced to six years' imprisonment with hard labour together with fifteen strokes with a leather strap.

So, instead of the Ordinance having wiped out the 'Black Peril', the situation remained the same as it had before the Ordinance was passed. But now the town was crystallising

90

into two separate, self-conscious worlds and was experiencing a depression which Hubert Murray described as a 'period of almost unrelieved misfortune'.[5]

Even before the economic depression hit the capitalist world in 1929 and affected even the remote Pacific, coconut and rubber prices began to fall. Gold, which had yielded Papua a large revenue, fell off badly between 1926 and 1930. Copra, Papua's main crop, fell very low on the world market. Only a Commonwealth duty in favour of Papua's rubber saved that industry from collapse. Shipping fell away so much that the three local shipping companies formed a pool to eliminate wasteful competition, limit tonnage and avoid a price war. Whitten Bros., one of the oldest established firms in Port Moresby, whose store had stood near the corner of Musgrave and Douglas streets since the beginning of the century went out of business.

Work was hard for both whites and blacks to find. Salaries were reduced. In 1932 public service salaries were reduced by 10 per cent and in 1933 Steamships Trading Company reduced all salaries by 20 per cent. People could not afford their usual pleasures: in 1932-3 the imports of ale, spirits and beverages fell to a little more than half what they had been the year before. Government revenue too was affected, made up as it was of a grant from the Commonwealth (£50,000) and of customs and excise charges, of postage stamp revenue and of an export tax on copra which slid up and down according to the world price. By 1930-1, the Lieutenant-Governor reported that almost every item of revenue had declined. Very drastic cuts in government expenditure were made and an economy drive was begun. To make matters worse, the Commonwealth subsidy was cut by £5000. It was not until 1934 that copra and rubber prices began to rise again. During the 1920s and 1930s the economic difficulties of the white residents exacerbated their relations both with the Papuans and with the Lieutenant-Governor who, they considered, acted always in the interests of the Papuans. Caroline Ralston has observed that in the Pacific beach communities 'any commercial difficulty or embarrassment suffered by the Europeans caused discord' and 'brought into the open latent attitudes and expressions of white superiority'.[6] In Port Moresby this phenomenon soon became evident.

The new self-consciousness among the Papuans who lived in or near the town was seen during June 1929 when Charles Abel brought his Kwato XI of 'native cricketers' to Port Moresby to play the local white team. The Kwato XI, captained by Charles's son Cecil Abel, was an experienced team which had already played whites in Samarai. Its reputation for skilful cricket preceded it and the Moresby players were urged to practise in the hope of being selected to play Kwato. The match was a singular event. The European population of Port Moresby turned out to watch and the match 'sent every other topic out of sight at the week-end.'[7] Even more singular was the great number of natives from villages near and far who came too. H. L. Murray, Official Secretary, in a report of the match, realised its importance. 'The match furnished pleasing evidence of the awakening of the Papuan to a broader racial sense of pride.' It was obvious 'from the interest and excitement of natives from all parts of the Territory that the Kwato team was regarded as representing the Papuans as a whole, and that Kiwais, Orokaivas and others took the same pride in the skill of the Kwato cricketers as the Samarai natives themselves'.[8] This was a new phenomenon. It was obvious too that the white residents regarded their team as representing the white man..It was a kind of Test Match between black and white. Grant, a Port Moresby player, was described as hitting 'the first white sixer of the match'. The *Courier* devoted almost two whole pages in two successive issues to an account of the match which was won, but only narrowly, by the white team after a tense last day when it seemed that Kwato might be victorious. Both sides 'battled their hardest for victory', and, as in a Test Match, the selectors were blamed for the near defeat of the Moresby team.

The 'broader sense of racial pride' which made Papuans see themselves as a group was pleasing to some whites, for it was now possible to engage in contest with them, though not on equal terms. At the official dinner at the Papuan hotel given by the victorious Papuan Cricket Club, the President, rising to support the toast to Cricket, said that he hoped that some day the Port Moresby team 'could play with the black men and realise that they were playing with gentlemen. He hoped that some day they could sit down with them at the same board.' Only the two white members of the Kwato team were present at the dinner and Charles Abel, the manager, replied for the other players, none of whom was present at the dinner. He told the company that 'it could not afford to despise the native, and must make the best of him. One way to transform their character was to put them into cricket.'

Playing cricket was both a way of Europeanising the Papuan and—in such contests between black and white teams—a way of containing aggression within harmless and permissible bounds. It was not so easy to contain sexual aggression. Peeping into bathrooms or bedrooms and other such expressions of curiosity; touching and feeling and attempting to make sexual advances towards women, and other such expressions of sexual aggression; all continued in Port Moresby and were not prevented even by threat of the most drastic punishment.

In October 1929, not three years after the passage of the White Women's Protection Ordinance, two well known Port Moresby women reported being assaulted in the night at their houses on Paga Hill. The more serious attack was reported by the wife of one of the town's leading merchants, a man who had been at the head of the anti-Murray campaign in 1920-1. She had been asleep late on the night of 31 October when she was 'awakened by a native crawling on top of her in bed'. He 'did not cause her any bodily injury, but tried to place his arm around her neck when attempting to lie on top of her'.[9] The other woman had some days earlier been awakened by 'someone touching her hand'.[10] Neither woman rang the police. The first woman's experience was not reported to the European constable until 11.00 a.m. on the following morning and the second not until five days after the event, for which tardiness they were criticised by police and government. They did not raise the alarm though Paga Hill was one of the three areas of the town nightly covered by two members of the Town Guard on beat duty. All night, two armed native constables patrolled the area from 'Mr. Pearson's corner in Musgrave street, hence to Port Road, along Port Road to Paga Point (Mr. Baldie's residence) back again around Paia Hill to Mr. Hilder's residence, thence back to the corner of the Public Works buildings, thence along Douglas Street to point of commencement'.[11] A shout from either woman might have brought the constables. Why did the two women do nothing immediately, it was asked.

Perhaps they had no faith in the Armed Native Constabulary. Perhaps as no physical damage had been done, they saw no reason to shout. Perhaps they were shocked and feared the humiliation of public knowledge and the possible slander—there were those who might say that they must have provoked the attack; perhaps they were prepared to forget the incidents, but their husbands saw it as a political matter of some importance. One woman brought her case to the Central Court. The other did not. Her case may or may not have been dealt with in the magistrate's court.[12] The lack of court records is particularly tantalising in these cases for not only is there only a sketchy account of what both men did, but without records it is not possible to make any judgments on the questions raised above.

The day after he had received a report on these two cases, Murray sent a radiogram to the Prime Minister, while the town soon heard of the attacks. E. A. James expressed in the *Courier* the horror and fear of many of the white residents for 'this class of crime which is perhaps the most serious that could possibly be imagined in a country such as this'. As Port buzzed with these two cases, yet another was reported in the press. On this occasion the frightened woman, who had been awakened by a man catching hold of her, gave the alarm; the police were rung and within a few minutes the Headquarters Officer Leonard Logan with all the available police had cordoned off the road to the Village and to Badili. The Town Guard then moved towards Lawes Road on the Ela beach side and caught a man, distressed and panting, who had emerged from the grass and quickly tried to hide. He later made a statement and was charged under section 3 of the White Women's Protection Ordinance with attempted rape. Nine days after his arrest, the prisoner, a

94

Delta Division man, had passed—without counsel—through both the Magistrate's Court and the Central Court and was found guilty of indecent assault. He was sentenced by Judge Gore to ten years' imprisonment with hard labour.

Here was a series indeed. The White Women's Protection Ordinance had been passed precisely to put an end to such attacks. Was it to prove a harmless and useless threat? One resident said that it had—and worse—in a letter to the *Courier*. The Act had proved to be 'a dismal and miserable failure and could more suitably be called the "White Women's Persecution Act".' It was unsafe, said the writer, to leave 'one's womenfolk' for five minutes alone with a native, day or night. For a white woman to have to fight a native to preserve her honour was 'a blot on any British settlement' and something would have to be done 'to give the honour due to God's greatest gift, a white woman'. E. A. James declared in an editorial that 'the present problem of natives' attacks on white women was the result of lack of control over the natives in the Territory, and insolence unpunished causing a general feeling of contempt for the white race'.

While the latest case was being heard, a house servant known as Miaro appeared before the Magistrate's Court on a charge of the attempted rape of the merchant's wife on 31 October. A Gulf man, Miaro came from Motu Motu, one of two large Toaripi villages at the mouth of the Lakekamu River. The Crown was represented in the Magistrate's Court by its prosecutor E. B. Bignold. Miaro, so it was reported in the *Courier*, 'reserved his defence' but what this defence was, it is impossible to discover since on this occasion the *Courier* did not report the case when it came to the Central Court on the grounds that white women should be protected against publicity in these cases.[13] The *Courier* reported in some detail the later cases involving the judge's wife—against its stated policy—but was reticent on the merchant's.

Miaro, who was not defended, was charged under section 3 of the White Women's Protection Ordinance and as witnesses against him the Crown called two prisoners, Karo and Kore, who were brought from Badili gaol to give evidence of 'certain admissions'.[14] Karo, whose father was from

Miaro's village of Motu Motu and whose mother was from Hula, was formerly a member of the Armed Native Constabulary. Arrested for the murder of his fellow policeman while the two were escorting mail from Port to Kokoda, he was found guilty of manslaughter and sentenced to seven years' imprisonment. After his term had expired, he returned to Hula where he was again arrested, this time for the robbery of a safe containing about £120 from the Rigo government station. He was sentenced to ten years' imprisonment.[15] It was during his first term of imprisonment that he was brought out to give evidence against Miaro. Six months after Miaro's case, the same pair of prisoners appeared again in the Central Court to give 'evidence of certain admissions' against a man, accused of grabbing hold of the judge's wife while she slept. On this occasion the case was reported in the *Courier*, so we learn that the accused claimed Karo was lying. Eight years later, while still a prisoner at Badili, Karo was convicted of the murder of a prison warder and his wife and child. Like the two men whom he had helped to convict in 1930, Karo was not represented by counsel; his own admission and prison witnesses were evidence against him.

Miaro's case lasted all day Friday and half of Saturday, after which Mr Justice Gore pronounced him guilty of attempted rape under section 3 of the White Women's Protection Ordinance, for which the only possible sentence was death. The *Courier*'s brief report of the sentence on the following Friday was headed:[16]

NATIVE
To be
Hanged

When the Executive Council met on 6 January to confirm the sentence and order the execution, the Government Secretary, H. W. Champion, and the Commissioner for Native Affairs, J. T. O'Malley, dissented from the Council's approval of the death sentence on the grounds that the evidence 'though sufficient to establish an indecent assault is not sufficient to establish beyond reasonable doubt an attempt to commit rape'.[17] They must have been swayed by the nature of the penalty for attempted rape, for it is hard to imagine what else the accused man was trying to do.

Murray had it in his power to grant either a pardon or remission of sentence and in the light of the dissent by such senior members of the Council had legitimate reasons to do so. But he did not, and the death sentence was confirmed. The Executive Council ordered that it be carried out on the following Monday morning, 13 January, at Badili gaol and after the meeting this information was radioed to the Prime Minister of Australia.

Preparations for the execution were made at Badili gaol; the gibbet was erected and the town waited for the execution which, once and for all, would show that the government seriously intended to punish those who attacked white women and put a stop to the attacks. The morning of 13 January dawned, but to the surprise and dismay of Port residents, no execution took place. The day before the execution Murray had received the following telegram from the Australian Prime Minister, J. H. Scullin:

> Your telegram of 6th January. In view of the lack of unanimity in Executive Council, one dissentient being the Commissioner for Native Affairs, and on general grounds, Prime Minister makes strongest possible representations that proposed execution of native offender be not proceeded with.[18]

The Labor party, which had been in power since October 1929, was opposed to capital punishment and in Australia, the death sentence was always commuted in Federal territories while the Scullin government was in power. It had not the power automatically to do this in Papua, and could only request that the Lieutenant-Governor exercise his power under the Papua Act to grant a reprieve. Murray had expected the request to reprieve, he told the Prime Minister, because of the opposition of two such senior members of the Executive Council, which is perhaps why he dodged the issue himself, even though he thought the evidence convincing.[19] He wrote to his sister-in-law, Lady Mary Murray, on the day the execution was to have taken place: 'I suppose he ought to have been hanged, but I was glad to fall in with the Prime Minister's request. We have not had an execution for many years.'[20] This feeling was mixed with a resentment against the Australian Government for taking the choice away from him, but he never expressed either feeling publicly. Rightly foreseeing that the citizens would turn with anger on him when deprived of Miaro, Murray sought permission from the Commonwealth Government to publish the Prime Minister's telegram; and on the morning of the execution, before announcing the reprieve, sent a car to Badili gaol to collect Miaro and drive him to Sapphire creek, thence to go under armed guard to a gaol at Kokoda. It was a masterly stroke, which almost failed when Miaro escaped from custody in the rough country on the Kokoda track.

After Miaro had been whisked away, Murray informed the residents that the execution would not take place that morning because of 'representations from the Commonwealth' adding that the Executive Council would meet to discuss the representations. The Council met on the afternoon of the execution day and made an order that the death sentence be commuted to life imprisonment in hard labour. Miaro had been gone from Port since very early morning.[21]

Then the storm broke in Port Moresby with a fury and a hysteria greater than that of 1925, aggravated by Murray's dictatorial manner of proceeding and by the incredible accident of Miaro's escape. There was a race to recapture him. Murray wrote to Lady Mary Murray on that day, 'I was afraid lest he should be lynched if the white residents got hold of him.' It was clear to the *Papuan Courier*, which reported the whole sequence of events that day to its readers, that the Executive Council meeting was a farce and its decision a foregone conclusion, since Miaro had already been removed from Badili gaol before the meeting. The reporter bitterly commented on Miaro's escape that he supposed he would be 'charged for this escapade and another fortnight added to his life holiday, all at public expense'. Editorially, the *Courier* was very belligerent. In a finely rhetorical statement, James set out the history of the White Women's Protection Ordinance, estimating the number of attacks on white women since it had come into force as over thirty (in fact, eleven cases had come before the Central Court in this time). He alleged that while several men had been committed on a capital charge in the magistrate's court 'for some reason, in every case, the charge was reduced in the Central Court'.

Why had not the government agreed to the residents' demands for more European police? What *were* these 'representations' of the Commonwealth Government? What had the Lieutenant-Governor said in his telegram to the Prime Minister? 'Mr. Scullin and his party live a long way off' said James. 'Their womenfolk are in no danger of being outraged by neolithic savages. They know nothing of the matter.' If the Executive Council had had any strength, if it really represented the white residents, it would have told Mr Scullin this and resigned in a body rather than be overruled in this case. What would be the effect of this reprieve on 'the native mind'? James could only guess that 'the pleasant publicity which Miaro has received will encourage others to follow his path'. 'Consider', James thundered, 'that now after twenty-four years of Australian rule no white woman is safe in Port Moresby unless she locks herself in a cage.'[22]

The blame for this state of affairs was easy to pin home, for the 'feeble vacillating efforts of the Government to deal with the problem are now exposed in all their nakedness'. His Excellency had been quite wrong. The knowledge of the death penalty was not enough to deter attackers of white women. The residents had known all along that threats were not enough, that action was needed. Now was the time for action. Every man was grimly conscious, said the *Courier*, that unless something was done, it was the bounden duty of the white man to take charge. White men would, if necessary, have an executive of their own, police the town themselves and comb out the natives who had no right to be there. 'We have lost all confidence in the existing Government.'[23]

As in 1925, public opinion was both mirrored and manufactured in the *Courier*. Several unsigned letters which appeared supporting the editorial statement were perhaps genuine, perhaps written in the office, but whether or not, only two letters in opposition were published. Nearly all letters which ever appeared in the *Courier* were pseudonymous. In a small town this is not surprising. 'An Australian' and 'Reprieve' joined the editorial attack on the same day as the editorial. 'In Papua an outpost of the British Empire, white women are allowed to be ravished by natives—while men, or so-called men, look calmly on wondering in all probability who the next one will be', wrote 'Australian' and demanded a change of administration. 'Reprieve' thought that the death penalty *had* reduced crime, but that after Miaro's reprieve the 'grinning Gulf natives [were] beginning to throw out their chests as much as to say that they can do as they please as they are immune from punishment'.[24] The Commonwealth Government had done irreparable harm in undoing the good work which the Papuan Government had achieved by passing the White Women's Protection Ordinance.

The following Friday's *Courier* carried six letters on the Miaro case plus an editorial attacking the government. The only one of these letters to bear a signature came from a white woman, Mrs Vieusseux, a Port Moresby transport operator. The others came from 'Junius Junior', 'Reason', 'Doubtful', 'Femino' and 'Pale Liver'. 'Doubtful', quoting the Sydney *Bulletin*, gave figures to show that in the United States, where few murders were followed by executions, the crime rate was high, but in England, where capital punishment was always inflicted, murder was much less common. Mrs Vieusseux thought that the Commonwealth Government had no right to interfere in matters which it did not understand, especially since the Papuan Government—erring on the side of leniency to natives as it did—would never have agreed to the death sentence had it not been necessary. She thought herself that public whipping would do 'more permanent good than all the long sentences of imprisonment'.

E. A. James and the other residents, with the *Courier* as their forum, used the Miaro case to agitate against the Murray administration; James revived his demand for elected rather than appointed non-official members of the Legislative and Executive Councils. In the words of L. H. Hilder, clerk of the Executive Council, the whole matter soon 'degenerated into a diatribe against the Lieutenant-Governor and the Executive Council'.

The residents exaggerated the dangers to white women. Murray, through his supporters, attacked the residents but himself made no statement; neither did he show them the telegram from the Commonwealth Government, perhaps considering that the information about the two Council members who had opposed the death penalty was dangerous. James and his letter writers played on the basic emotions of fear and lust, James even suggesting that it would not be long 'before those native policemen become a menace themselves', thus depriving the residents of any feeling of security they might have had and undermining the whole basis of Murray's law. They called for the most violent solutions; for lynch law. 'It is the stern duty of every husband and father, aye, and every white man' wrote 'Femino',[25] 'to see that this matter is not allowed to pass into oblivion. White men of this Territory! Rouse yourselves— don't think so much of your little jobs. Be men and prove yourself [sic] as such by protecting your womenfolk, even if you have to take the law into your own hands.' 'F.E.T.' favoured flogging; he suggested it for 'every native reported for insolence, or attempted assault on any white woman'. The advantage of a flogging is that it is 'clean, most effective and does not leave any dirty stains'. 'I regret to inform you that the agitation shows no sign of abatement' wrote Murray to the Prime Minister on 6 February, 'residents are still busily engaged in frightening one another, and the local newspaper is no less busily engaged in frightening them all'.[26] He had a short respite from some of the furore when in Sydney on 20 February 1930 he took himself a second wife, Mrs Mildred Vernon, an Irish widow, a marriage which would provide him little comfort.

Among this 'display of ignorance, blood-lust and egotistical nonsense', which was how J. T. Bensted, Director of Public Works, described the letters, three voices spoke more calmly; they advocated neither lynching nor flogging nor even capital punishment. Two of these voices belonged to the government: one was J. T. Bensted's own, the other was that of L. H. Hilder, clerk of the Executive Council. The third belonged to the town's only private solicitor, R. D. Bertie. Bertie published the view—which he feared might prove novel to *Courier* readers—that heavy punishments had never caused a decrease in crime. 'If terror could have prevented crime', he said, 'crime would have long ceased to exist.' He urged more police, under European supervision, and the appointment of a capable magistrate whose only task would be 'to watch over the natives'. All men agreed that the attacks were serious and had to stop; the question only was how it was to be done and how the offenders ought to be dealt with and whether prevention was more important than abuse of the Murray administration. L. H. Hilder drew up a five point policy of prevention:

1. A Town Guard, independent of the Constabulary, ought to be set up, either composed of 'Local Natives or Kiwais'.
2. Householders should be issued with police whistles.
3. Employers were to issue special numbered cardboard permits if natives were out of their premises after 9 pm.
4. An electrical device operated by a button could be placed on beds and when activated it would simultaneously sound the alarm and let off a flare.

And the fifth proposal was that 'Gulf natives', being a 'thoroughly bad lot', should be kept outside the town boundary in compounds after nightfall 'and a roll call should be made at 9 o'clock each evening'.

Bensted, on six months' furlough before retirement, believed that example, and not punitive laws, was the answer to these attacks. Explanation and a good example from whites, with harsh laws as a deterrent only in the most extreme cases, were the government's proposals. If Murray and his supporters had had their way, the Government Secretary's proposal that no native should be allowed in the township of Port Moresby between the hours of say 10 p.m. and 6 a.m., except Armed Constables and hospital orderlies on duty and perhaps some others would have been put into practice. The employers would in this case have had to provide housing for their servants outside the town boundaries and they would not have had the use of servants over dinner. The Government Secretary and the Lieutenant-Governor thought that such a law would have made the commission of sexual offences without detection practically impossible and suggested to the Australian Government that the residents, by putting convenience before the safety of their women, showed that they were not as concerned at the danger as they pretended.[27]

The government tried another way of dealing with the problem, by explanation to Papuans literate in English, through the *Papuan Villager*, the educational newspaper for Papuans edited and written by the Government Anthropologist, F. E. Williams. Readers were told in the first issue that it was 'not for white men (they have a paper of their own). It is for the brown men.' Written in English, 'because the Government wants you to learn the white man's language', the paper was paid for from the Native Education Fund which came solely from native taxation. In the first issue Williams also explained to Papuans that they would have to buy the paper, 'just as the white man must pay for his paper'. So they paid for it twice, once as taxpayers and once as purchasers. In this journal the government educated Papuans in those ways of white society which it wished them to emulate and reminded them of those parts of their cultural heritage which it did not wish them to forget. The January 1930 issue reported two cases of assault upon white women which had brought the death sentence and ten years' hard labour and added this warning: 'All Papuan natives have to know that white women are sacred and must not be interfered with. There is no stronger *taravatu*, or law, in this land.' The provisions of the White Women's Protection Ordinance followed, together with this conclusion: 'These are strong laws. But there are some bad natives, and the white women must be kept safe.'

Despite the solemn, calming government voice, the fear and fury did not abate and demands for more severe punishment continued, together with demands for more severe regulation of natives in the town. As in 1926, new regulations framed and put into operation were aimed at keeping Papuans out of the way of whites. The 'Gulf native' as we have already seen, received an early reputation for venery. Four out of the eight convicted offenders under the White Women's Protection Ordinance were natives of the Gulf or Delta Divisions and this was enough to prove the residents' fears of these 'grinning Gulf natives'. The possibility that most offenders were Gulf or Delta men because most domestic servants were Gulf or Delta men and most offenders were domestic servants was not entertained by the residents, though it was by Murray,[28] who nevertheless had a regulation brought into the Executive Council under which 'Gulf Natives'—in practice any western men—were prohibited from signing on as domestics out of their own division. Port Moresby residents who had Gulf houseboys were 'invited to apply to have their contracts cancelled and to send them home.'[29] It is not known whether anyone took advantage of this offer. Dr Strong dissented on the Council: 'I think it unfair both to the natives and to the employers to forbid boys to work in Port Moresby who have committed no offence.'[30]

To enforce the rule about 'foreign natives' staying out of the town, new rules were gazetted making it an offence to return to the town within six months of being sent back to the village. The penalty was six months' imprisonment with hard labour; a 'foreign native' who had been imprisoned in his own district and then came into a town suffered the same penalty if he were caught there.

The Resident Magistrate of the Gulf Division, G. H. Massey Baker, blamed the Port for its corruption of Gulf men. 'No one here thinks of employing a boy who has worked in Port Moresby if he can help it. It is the first thing we ask an applicant for a job. If he says he worked in Port for so long and for so and so, he is told to get out. Two or three are not allowed inside my station fence even if they want to sell nuts, under pain of getting a charge of No. 8 shot.'[31]

Passing these regulations was as far as the government would go for the moment, but it was not far enough for some residents. More letters appeared in the *Courier* and James kept up his campaign, attacking the government and whipping up the residents. Some of the letters gave evidence to support Murray's action in the Miaro case. As he wrote to the Prime Minister in April: 'I avoided the danger of lynching by sending this prisoner out of Port Moresby secretly, and some hours before the time fixed for the execution; but this ruse may not succeed on another occasion.'[32] This extract appeared in a letter in the *Papuan Courier* on 14 February 1930, headed 'The Black Horror':

104

One of the most disquieting things about the above menace to our womenfolk and the part played by the Authorities is that, practically all if not all these offences have been committed under the shadow of the Police Stations. It means, and the nigger knows it, there is protection for him, following his act even, and, no protection for the victim. . . .

KLU [*sic*] KLUX

So dissatisfied were the residents that they again resorted to their traditional methods of agitating. On 1 April 1930, a group of influential male residents of Port Moresby met in the office of G. A. Loudon, manager of the British New Guinea Development Company, and an old and formidable enemy of Sir Hubert Murray.[33] The group was described in the *Courier* as a General Committee interested in the Protection of White Women from molestation by natives, and its members were said to be 'representatives of the towns-people of Port Moresby.' They were all members of the town's commercial interests and for the most part were old timers in Papua, many of whom had been active in the Chamber of Commerce and Residents' Association in 1920-1.

Loudon was chairman of the meeting. The others present were Captain A. S. Fitch; W. Dupain, manager of Burns Philp; R. S. Goodyear; J. R. Clay; E. P. Mahony, manager of the Port Moresby Freezing Company; E. J. Frame, a former employee of E. J. Whitten for nineteen years and then with the B.N.G. Development Company; R. D. Bertie; Lewis Lett; J. McDonald, former head gaoler and works supervisor; E. A. James, owner and editor of the *Papuan Courier*, accountant and auditor; N. Calcutt, manager of the Bank of New South Wales; E. F. Whitten, owner and founder of Whitten Bros. Ltd, merchants and customs agents; O. D. Scafer, manager of the Port Moresby branch of Whitten Bros.; and R. S. Munro, a building contractor.

Loudon asked each member of the General Committee to submit views about causes and cures so that these could be presented to His Excellency who would be asked to meet the group in a conference. Murray agreed to meet the group on Friday 4 April, on condition that the representative of the Press was not present. In the two intervening days,

Loudon prepared a paper containing the views of the committee and about fifteen men took it along to Murray's office. This must have been the deputation which Lett wrongly described as taking place in 1925. James, excluded from the confrontation which he had done so much to bring about, kept up his campaign of alarm. On the day of the deputation he published a story about two more attempts to commit indecent assault under the heading: 'More Assaults by Natives on White Women'. These were two cases of assault, one not brought to the Central Court, which the paper linked with the reprieve of Miaro.

The deputation presented its paper to the Lieutenant-Governor. The paper began by stating the credentials of the deputation:

> As a deputation we do not propose to represent the Public Service or the Mission Interests in the Territory, as both of these are already represented in the Legislative Council, but we claim that our Meeting of 15 citizens of Port Moresby is representative of every clean living resident in the Territory.

It then stated that it considered the recent cases of assault upon white women to be 'a direct result of the Prime Minister's interference in the sentence of [MIARO],' and urged the Lieutenant-Governor to send a protest to the Prime Minister.

The members outlined what they believed to be the causes of the present 'serious situation'. Dismissing the argument that a cause could be ignorance of the provisions of the Ordinance, since its objects and penalties had been carefully explained, they considered that the provisions of the Ordinance were not 'sufficiently severe in the case of criminal trespass or intent'. They believed also that natives, unable to satisfy their sexual desires by buying women since they were paid a lump sum at the end of their contract of service, attacked white women. They believed gaol discipline to be so lax that natives boasted of their exploits with white women to other prisoners who then emulated them. Finally, they thought that the effect of motion pictures on natives could well be harmful.

What ought to be done? First, and above all, the men

of the deputation proposed: 'That natives must be taught that this is a European Town and not a native playground.' Then followed detailed proposals. The powers of the government to deport European or native undesirables should be reviewed and either made wider or be interpreted more flexibly. This may have been a reference to those European women who were thought to be encouraging native men or to the European men who joked in a racy, masculine way with their servants. Both types were attacked in the local press. All natives should be removed from the town at night; no passes should be granted by employers to move around town after 9 p.m. except in extreme urgency; women sleeping without 'adequate male protection' should be provided with police protection; bicycles should be issued to policemen. 'We suggest', the paper stated,

> That additional penalties should provide that any native convicted and imprisoned should be first publicly flogged. Similar instruments to be used as when flogging a white man in other countries, viz., cat and triangle.
> That in any proved attempt emasculation be automatic unless the death penalty has been imposed.

The public could assist the authorities by allowing police to search native premises and by immediately reporting any case of assault; in fact the deputation thought that failure to report an assault, an attempted assault or a trespass, ought itself to constitute an offence. The public could also assist the authorities by 'inviting the co-operation of lady residents to advise, through a committee, new arrivals to the Territory, and others if necessary, as to their conduct and treatment of natives,'[35] a delicate and veiled reference to the conduct of women as a cause of attack, despite the fact that none of the females whose cases we have dealt with were ladies with towels. The Matron had been walking along a public street, the nurse was asleep at the hospital, the judge's wife was standing on the verandah of her own house and on the second occasion was asleep in her bed, the merchant's wife was asleep in her bed and so were the women in several of the other cases. The child was three years old. There are several cases for which there is no information, but in those which were best known and caused the most commotion, there is no evidence that the attacks were in any way the fault of the victims' provocative or careless behaviour.

The final proposals were for the establishment of a police constable at Koke and the installation around the town and at the police station of beach alarms so that police and residents might be quickly put on the alert in cases of attack. James could print only what he was given by the other members of the committee, but he kept the pot boiling by publishing his own suggestions in the event that they had not been included in the paper presented to Murray. He urged that a non-official member 'acceptable to the white residents' be appointed to the Executive Council, presumably to stiffen up that body; but this was an Aunt Sally since the residents could have had such a member since the 1924 amendments to the Papua Act if they had agreed to put up a candidate. He urged that legislation be drawn up making 'insolence of natives to Europeans a punishable offence . . . It must necessarily follow', he said, 'that insolence will breed contempt, and from that springs the more serious offences.'[36] This proposal had not been included in the Committee's paper.

Murray was in a difficult position. Disappointed in the behaviour of the native people,[37] attacked by the white residents for the reprieve of Miaro—a decision not his own —his authority as Lieutenant-Governor was being undermined by the Australian Government. Scullin 'has been very queer too about capital punishment', he wrote to his brother, 'it is really my responsibility, not his, whether a death sentence is carried out, but he makes me refer all the cases with the evidence to him, for his decision. In fact, he treats me as if I were a departmental officer'.[38]

On the one hand Murray disagreed with the residents' conviction that more severe punishments would prevent sexual attacks and disliked their hysteria and exaggeration; but on the other he wanted to convince the Labor prime minister that he knew the situation in Port Moresby and that he should be allowed to impose the death penalty there. 'I think there can be no doubt', he wrote to Scullin, 'that there is a real deepseated feeling of alarm lest sentences passed by Papuan Courts should be remitted or mitigated in Australia.' On this occasion he was far more in sympathy with the residents than he had been in 1925 when they presented their petition, as he wrote in the same despatch, sent on the day after he had received the deputation:

I wish to emphasize the facts that (even allowing for hysteria and exaggeration) residents are genuinely upset by the danger to which their wives and daughters are exposed, and that there is a great difference between a white man's country like Australia, where capital punishment is probably not necessary, and the territory of Papua, where a small white community is surrounded by a barbaric population hardly out of the stone age, and in which capital punishment, hateful as it must be to any man of humane instincts, is really a necessary condition of safety.[39]

During the meeting of 4 April, the members of the deputation had found Murray courteous and considerate of several of their suggestions. He persuaded the deputation that emasculation and public flogging with cat and triangle 'could not be acted upon in an Australian territory',[40] and that they were weakening their case by insisting on these remedies. After some days he arranged a further meeting, this time with the Executive Council and five members of the General Committee: Whitten, Lett, Frame, Goodyear and Bertie during which 'most satisfactory' discussions were held.

Two weeks later the government made public those of the Committee's proposals it had accepted. It had not agreed to the demands for harsher punishments: there would be no castration and no public flogging. What Murray did agree to were measures for the stricter supervision of Papuans in the town. He privately believed some of the measures 'rather futile' but considered it better 'under the circumstances, to accept any suggestions that might be offered, so far as they were not absolutely objectionable'.[41]

He had agreed to appoint an intelligence officer whose job it would be 'to get into close contact with natives in and near Port Moresby, obtain information for the police and keep all suspects under supervision'.[42] He had agreed to provide bicycles and a dinghy for the night guard and police whistles for the residents. He had agreed to give the right of search without warrant to the European policeman at all times and to native police only under certain specified conditions. The way in which this provision was described varied according to its intended readers. In writing to the Australian Prime Minister Murray described the measure thus: 'Power is being given to European police, and in certain circumstances, to native police, to enter the native quarters on any premises.'[43] Here the harsh fact of search without warrant is obscured by the words 'to enter'. Native police may enter 'in certain circumstances' but the circumstances are not specified. The places which police may enter are described as 'native quarters or premises'. The whole thing is vague and the language formal.

In the Executive Council minutes where there was no need to allay fears either of un-Australian measures or race-prejudiced actions, the details were spelt out and in the ordinary language of the colonial Australians:

> It was ordered that the C.L.O. [Crown Law Office] be asked to draft a Bill giving power to an European officer of Police to enter a boys house at any time of the day or night, and any A.N.C. the same power after an offence of assault or trespass has been reported to the Police.[44]

Murray had agreed that employers should be required to give particulars of all natives lodged in their premises at night, and that all natives convicted of sexual offences should be sent to one remote gaol, probably at Daru, an island in the mouth of the Fly river. And he agreed in principle to the ultimate symbolic proposal of the Committee, that a fence be built across the town from the harbour to Ela beach, along Lawes Road. The government added some decisions of its own. It appointed nine extra police constables to the Town Guard, increasing it from twelve to twenty-one men, and suggested that a line of lights along the proposed fence might be useful.[45]

While these negotiations were going on between the Committee and the government, the residents circulated a petition addressed to the Prime Minister of Australia. Signed by ninety-two male white residents, mostly from the Chamber of Commerce, the petition 'quietly and respectfully' expressed concern at the reprieve and made common cause with the colonial government. After sketching the history of the White Women's Protection Ordinance, the petition concluded:

> We would press on you that it is not a matter of general policy in dealing with the native population, but a question of dealing with a local trouble, and the experience of our Lieutenant Governor and his Council in such a matter should make their opinion final and conclusive.
>
> We therefore wish to protest very respectfully but very earnestly against the interference by the Federal Authorities with the considered decision of the Lieutenant Governor and Executive Council in this case.[46]

This petition, dated 28 April, was forwarded with a covering note from His Excellency in June. There was no word about it in the *Courier*; James having no need to whip up either support for or antagonism against Murray.

That Port Moresby was a white man's town was never more piquantly displayed than in the appointment of the intelligence officer, surely the only spy whose appointment, name and rank have been published in the local press. He was W. M. Rich, Assistant Resident Magistrate at Losuia. Born in Papua, son of the L.M.S. missionary at Fife Bay in the Eastern Division, he spoke two Papuan languages. The *Papuan Courier* briefed everyone who could read English on these facts of his life and also on his movements. 'We understand that instructions recalling him have already been forwarded to Losuia', it reported, assuming, no doubt correctly, both that no Papuan ever read the white man's paper and that no white man would confide this news to a Papuan.

When the decisions of the government were communicated—on the same day—to the General Committee interested in the Protection of White Women from molestation by natives and to the Prime Minister of the Commonwealth, neither was completely satisfied. The Committee, in which James's voice was again heard, expressed its disappointment that some of the 'more important' suggestions had not been agreed to, particularly as these were the very suggestions

111

which represented 'the considered opinions of some of the older residents of the Territory, who have had the opportunity to study natives from other than the official angle'.[47] They asked the government to reconsider. It did, and found that there were still some proposals it could accept, among them being one to exclude offenders from the town.

It did this at the first sitting of the Legislative Council for 1930 when the Native Offenders' Exclusion Ordinance was brought forward. Short and clear, the Ordinance consisted of three parts only: the title, the statement of the offence and the penalty. It stated that 'no native convicted of any offence of an indecent nature against a white woman or girl shall upon discharge from custody come or remain within the boundaries of any town.' The penalty was imprisonment with hard labour for one year. As the Government Secretary introduced the Bill, he explained that excluded natives would be told about the new Ordinance and would have the town boundaries pointed out to them.

At the same meeting an amendment to the Police Offences Ordinance of 1912 was passed so that European officers of the Armed Native Constabulary were empowered to enter premises without warrant 'at any time of the day or night' in order to search 'that portion of the premises where native employees are housed'. Native members of the constabulary were empowered to search without warrant only 'on an assault or trespass being reported'. Each Bill passed through all its stages in as long as it took to move the suspension of standing orders, move the Bill, read it and vote on its clauses.

The Prime Minister would not at first approve the amendment to the Police Offences Act and sent it back to Murray. Search without warrant needed explaining to the Australian Government, and Murray explained it in a despatch. Since 'much of what these residents asked could not be approved by the Government . . . it was a relief when a request was made which was not only perfectly reasonable but also calculated to assist the administration of justice'.[48] The Minister approved.

The fence was talked about and approved but not, it seems, built. The Executive Council ordered that two

112

bicycles and five dozen police whistles be bought 'if necessary by telegram' and the government inserted the following advertisement in the *Papuan Courier* of 4 September 1930:

NOTICE
WHITE WOMEN'S
PROTECTION

Whistles, free of cost, to call the police guard in case of need, are available on application to the European constable. Applications from persons not connected with the telephone exchange will take priority.

H. W. Champion,
Gov. Sec.

The Headquarters Officer of the Armed Native Constabulary, Leonard Logan, received a special allowance to compensate for 'special additional police duties owing to the interference by natives with white women here; and to help police the town at night'.[49]

Both the increased security precautions and the further curtailing of that little freedom which Papuans had in the town were far more serious than Lett allows when he dismisses the fruits of the deputation as a 'dozen petty and quite useless precautions'.[50] While by no means petty, some of the precautions were less than useful.

Rich, the intelligence officer, had known many of Port Moresby's Suau and Motu speakers since childhood, so for a while he fared well and his work produced some practical results but it produced little in the way of a general explanation for attacks on white females. The practical results were simple. Rich reported that one of his informants had heard a Papuan, X, say that one day 'about four years ago' when he was in Sydney with his employer he 'had had three white women'. The employer of X was informed of this and told that he might cancel his servant's contract of service, but that, in any case, X would not be permitted to 'sign on' again. Two weeks later, X was paid off by his employer 'after a further report of a disrespectful reference by him to a European lady'. But what was the government to do with another report from Rich which told of a Papuan who told another that Mrs Z had asked him to come up to her house?

113

Nothing, as it turned out, except to express concern that 'some natives have an idea that they have quite a fair chance of inducing a white woman to have connexion with them and that it is worth while to take the risk'.[51] Inquiries were made about Mrs Z but nothing was found to her discredit.

At the same time that Rich was collecting information from his Port Moresby informants, the gaoler at Samarai with the help of Sergeant Bagita[52]—no mean spy—was collecting his own evidence from prisoners in his gaol. The gaoler's investigations revealed to him that attacks on white women were 'a sort of "pay-back" because a white man takes a Papuan female when he wants one and the men resent this'.[53] But Murray and Champion attached no importance to this explanation and said so to the Prime Minister when despatching the gaoler's report. Since they believed that attacks could be blamed on the careless behaviour of women who aroused the unrestrained passions of primitive males, their reaction was predictable and consistent, though irrational. Why the unrestrained passions of primitive males could not have been slaked more easily—and with less danger —upon Papuan women was a question they did not ask. And it was difficult, especially for humane white men who saw themselves as the protectors of Papuans, to believe that their charges had anything to resent. Rejecting the gaoler's explanations, the government waited for Rich's conclusions but he soon suffered the fate of all but the Philbys of espionage, and on 3 January Murray wrote to the Prime Minister reporting that Rich could no longer get anything from his informers. 'It has been found out that they have been reporting to Mr. Rich, and consequently no one will tell them anything.'[54]

Murray's variegated role as administrator of the Commonwealth's policy, head of a colonial government, spokesman for the white residents and benevolent protector of Papuans was spotlighted in the case of Miaro and the hysteria that surrounded his reprieve. The white residents, sure that the Commonwealth Government would never consent to the death penalty,[55] were concerned to show what evils this policy had led to in Papua. Every act, from Peeping Tom to murder, was alleged to be connected with the reprieve of Miaro. G. H. Massey-Baker wrote that the 'imprisonment of a fiend like [Miaro]'[56] with a lot of common criminals in one jail was bound to corrupt them all. The mood of some was expressed by a government servant who, after his wife had been disturbed twice in two weeks by a Papuan hand being put under her mosquito net and grabbing hold of her leg, determined that the next time the intruder came he would be prepared. He hoped, he told Murray in a letter, 'to hand over a corpse instead of the culprit'.[57] Someone did come and peered through her net. Drawing a knife from under her pillow, the wife struck at him and he got away. This man was warned by the government not to shoot the intruder but to leave matters to the law. He might well have greeted this advice with a hollow laugh since the law that had been passed was, in the eyes of the residents, a useless farce; that powerful deterrent they had won was now removed by the stubborn blindness of the Commonwealth Government and the weakness of their own.

In the year of Miaro's reprieve the Legislative Council, with one dissentient voice, passed this resolution of J. G. Nelsson:

> That this Council, while fully alive to the objection which any humane person must feel to capital punishment, is of the opinion, which it believes to be shared by the rest of the community, that the infliction of the death penalty is absolutely necessary in such cases as those for which it has been provided by the White Women's Protection Ordinance.[58]

The dissenting voice belonged to J. B. Clarke, Dauncey's replacement, who did not believe in capital punishment.

The white women took not much part in this campaign, though more than they had in the past. On the day that the first deputation met the Lieutenant-Governor, 'Prudence' published the following note in her social column: 'I hear the ladies of Papua are to be asked to sign a petition addressed to the Prime Minister of Australia, in connexion with the present native menace. This action, I understand, is being taken at the instance of Mrs. Jewell of Lolorua, and copies have been forwarded to Port Moresby and Samarai. The Port Moresby petition is at the *Courier* office and now open for signatures.'[59] The *Courier* promoted the petition, informing readers in the following week that it was being signed 'fairly rapidly in Port' but that there were still 'a number of signatures to be obtained'. 'Prudence' 'understood' that the petition would be sent along to anyone who could not get into the *Courier* office to sign it. 'We certainly want to get this completed and forwarded to its destination as soon as possible.'[60] Eighty-six women in Port Moresby, Samarai and environs signed the petition which began: 'We, the undersigned White Women, residents of Papua', continued with an account of the case of Miaro and concluded: 'In appealing to you, Sir, we are prompted only by feelings of humanity, and we firmly believe that one exemplary punishment would put an end to such crimes, and relieve us of the fearful apprehension in which we constantly live.'[61] The fears of the residents for the safety of white women were no doubt genuine. So was the concern about white prestige, white authority and the power of the colonial court and in these concerns, which formed a cause for this agitation of 1930, Murray and the residents were very much more united than in 1925.

The extent of the fear and anger aroused by each act of sexual aggression or possibility of aggression by a Papuan against a white woman was out of all proportion to the number of these attacks, just as the penalties exacted, especially under the White Women's Protection Ordinance, were out of all proportion to the seriousness of the attacks and to penalties for similar attacks on Papuan women. From 1925 to 1930, 154 Papuan males were charged in the Central Court with sexual offences against Papuan females; 141 were charged with rape. Of the remaining cases, three were charged with attempted rape, three with incest, two with carnal knowledge, two with indecent assault, one with attempted carnal knowledge, one with entering with intent and one with abduction. During the same period, twenty-two Papuans were charged in the same court with sexual offences against European females. Of these twenty-two cases, five were charged with being in a dwelling with intent, five with indecent assault, four with indecently dealing, five with attempted rape, two with being within curtilage, two with unlawfully dealing with a girl under fourteen, one with

116

attempted carnal knowledge and one with indecently annoying.

The conviction rate for Papuans accused of sexual offences against European females was far higher than for those accused of such offences against Papuan females. Of the twenty-two accused of the first sort of case, only three were found not guilty of any offence. In the case of the 154 charged with offences against Papuan females, eighty were found guilty of an offence and seventy-four not guilty.[62]

The sentences imposed on those convicted were altogether different in the two sorts of cases. The heaviest penalty for a Papuan convicted of a sexual assault on a Papuan female was four years' imprisonment with hard labour imposed on a Vailala man convicted in 1932 of the rape of a Pari girl at Bomana, near Port Moresby. Three years with hard labour was the sentence for the man who raped an old woman, and also for the eighteen plantation labourers convicted of the rape of one girl at Hisiu, a village close to their plantation. Twelve months with hard labour was the most common penalty for a Papuan male convicted of the rape of a Papuan female. The sentences passed on Papuan males convicted of offences against European females have already been mentioned. Fifteen of the twenty-two attacks against European females which came to the Central Court occurred in Port Moresby.

In the cases of attacks on white women which came to the Court in 1929 and 1930 the women had been able to protect themselves. By shouting for a husband or a servant, by shining a torch, by pushing off an intruder, the woman frightened away those who terrified or angered but did not hurt her. The judge's wife had first been peeped at, then visited by a man who caught hold of her mosquito net 'as if to lift it up';[63] another woman had been touched. Only the merchant's wife had woken to find a man lying on her and trying to clasp her round the neck. Despite the commotion of 1925 and 1926, despite the reprieve of Miaro and the cases of 1930, as Murray wrote to the Prime Minister, 'it is well to remember that there has never been a case of rape of a white woman in Papua'.[64] Certainly none had come before the Central Court.

Miaro owed his life to its being in the hands of his far away Labor party grandfathers in Australia rather than in those of his Port Moresby fathers. Despite all the arguments and petitions, the Commonwealth Government was not moved and on 28 June a cable was sent to Murray insisting that no death sentence be carried out before the Australian Government had considered it and made its representations. In August of the same year the Australian Acting Attorney-General prepared a case for confining the power to commute a death sentence in Papua and Norfolk Island to the Governor-General. This would have meant an amendment to their Acts.[65]

The mixture of panic, fear of blacks, anger, pique and the blow to local pride which his reprieve produced among the white residents of Port Moresby, together with the Lieutenant-Governor's belief that he ought not to have been overruled made Miaro's escape from the penalty of the White Women's Protection Ordinance a lucky one. The next Papuan to be sentenced to death under the Ordinance was not to be so lucky. His crime was worse, neither white residents nor Murray would have stood for another reprieve and, in the meantime, the Federal Labor Government had been defeated.

Five   Stephen

As the residents had succeeded in most of the demands which they had made on the government, and which the Australian Government would permit, public agitation about the danger to white women died down; but the passions which had erupted during the months after Miaro's reprieve kept boiling beneath the surface of public life in the town. 'One has to walk carefully', Murray had written to the Prime Minister in June 1930, 'as some of the residents are getting hysterical again', and the subject was never forgotten.[1] Murray sent reports about native attacks on white women to the Prime Minister with explanations and descriptions and justifications of his policy. All his despatches from 1930 emphasised the difference between conditions in Port Moresby and Australia and reminded the Prime Minister of the angry mood of the white residents which had followed Miaro's reprieve. Murray reported the case of the public servant, already quoted above, who threatened to bring the corpse of the next night prowler to the police station, together with the administration's warning against private and illegal punishments, but he added: 'I think it quite likely that we may at some time have a case in which a man has shot a native under circumstances in which such action could not be legally justified or excused. But whether he were justified or not no jury would convict him.'[2]

So the residents went about their business, protected by the increased guard of Armed Native Constables. The Armed Native Constabulary were in a very special way an arm of Murray's rule and a symbol of his methods. They were *his* police; they said so themselves for they wore 'Judge Murray's clothes'.[3] As much an army as a police force, the Armed Native Constabulary were issued with rifles, and the objects of their force were Papuans only; to Papuans they were the power of the *gavamani*. In some villages they were used by patrol officers and others to procure women, or they procured them for their own use; sometimes they exacted favours or influenced Papuans against 'signing-on'; sometimes they illegally recruited Papuans for private recruiters, sometimes they exacted reprisals against those Papuans who refused to carry for the government.[4] These were illegal acts for which policemen could be punished, but even performing their legal functions, they exercised much power.

White men were not arrested by members of the Armed Native Constabulary, nor did they expect to be. What had been the case in Monckton's time[5] remained the case as late as 1941, for when a brawl broke out in one of Moresby's two pubs the European policeman called on the public to help him control it. 'The native police are not used against Europeans', wrote *Pacific Islands Monthly*'s Port Moresby correspondent.[6]

Those residents who shared James's opposition to Sir Hubert Murray's native policy were likely to be impressed with James's doubts about the reliability of Murray's special force of native police. In March 1930, when two members of the Armed Native Constabulary were charged with the rape of the wives of fellow policemen, James made his position very clear in an editorial. 'That such charges can be made against two of the police upon whom the protection of the white women now depends' he wrote, 'is enough to shake whatever confidence they ever had in the Government's efforts to protect them.'[7]

It was not only Murray's opponents who had doubts. Murray himself had warned his outside men against expecting too much from the Armed Native Constabulary, and in particular against placing too much reliance upon the intelligence and self-control of N.C.Os. Officers 'should guard against this inclination which will probably be a source of disappointment and may possibly be a cause of disaster', he advised. But whatever Murray's misgivings about the Papuan 'character' and about the dangers of trusting natives, the members of the Armed Native Constabulary were a special group and a matter of pride and importance to the government. F. E. Williams continually publicised them and sang their praises in the *Papuan Villager*; they wore clothes on the upper parts of their bodies when this was forbidden to most

120

other Papuans; they were issued with rifles and were taught to use them and care for them; and they were given positions of trust and power. Murray was titular head of the Constabulary, and the Headquarters officer was in 1933 Leonard Logan, a man who had been a member of the Papuan service since 1921.

The highest rank to which a Papuan policeman could aspire was that of N.C.O.: sergeant major or sergeant. The only sergeant major in the force, until he died in 1933, was the legendary Simoi whose picture had adorned a Papuan stamp in 1932. Among the very few N.C.Os. was Stephen or Gorumbaru, promoted in 1931. Named Gorumbaru by his parents and Stephen by the Anglican mission which had educated him, he was sometimes known as Stephen Gorumbaru. He was from the Baniara district of the North Eastern Division. He had joined the Armed Constabulary in 1923, and by 1929 was out of the ruck. A photograph in the *Papuan Villager* during the Governor-General's tour of inspection of Papua showed Lord Stonehaven inspecting the Guard of Honour of native constables and Gorumbaru— then a corporal—was singled out by name in the accompanying text. This was no mean honour.

By 1932 some competence in English, arithmetic and general knowledge was required and examined before a constable could be promoted, though Police Motu was the *lingua franca* of the Armed Constabulary. An examination paper included the following questions: 'How many days are there in a year? How many Sundays are there in a year? How many ounces in a lb.? Give the names of the Gentlemen you know on the Council.' It also included three sums: one long division, one multiplication of a seven-figure number by a four-figure number and one addition of three eight-figure numbers. Not only could Stephen pass his promotion test but he could write well enough in English to contribute an article to the *Villager* in which he compared marriage in his own Division with marriage in Port Moresby and condemned the customary payment of bride wealth in the Central Division. In his area, he said, things were arranged differently, and better. There when a boy liked a girl and wanted to marry her they went to the priest who, after three weeks, married them. 'The boy married this girl: he never gave any payment to her father and mother, because we are N.E.D. people—our way! . . . Look on our first Adam and Eve. Did God make Adam and then gave £100 to pay for Eve to live with him?'[9] The size of the bridewealth payments also shocked him. 'We are not white staff, to earn £100 in a few months, or we got plenty of money in the bank to pay for our wives', he wrote. The practice should cease.

When he wrote this letter he was a member of the Headquarters Office at Konedobu, a select and trusted group which supplied the Town Guard, police for special patrols, police to guard the mail on its journey from Port to Buna along the track to Kokoda, police detailed for special duties with departmental officers on patrol, and twelve police permanently detailed as orderlies to government officers in Port Moresby; all positions of trust which also meant frequent direct and often intimate dealings with whites.

By 1933, this able and trusted policeman had risen to the rank of sergeant and to the wage of forty shillings a month— the highest wage to which a member of the Armed Native Constabulary could automatically rise—which put him into the upper ranks of Papuan wage earners. As a sergeant, on forty shillings a month, he was a member of a tiny upper crust in the Armed Native Constabulary; as a man he was one who had 'always borne a good character, both in the Mission and in his village, and who had had a long and meritorious record in the police.'[10] By now he was sometimes used by the Headquarters Officer as his own personal orderly and as the police barracks and the Headquarters Officer's residence were close by each other at Konedobu, it was natural that he should become friendly with the small daughter of the house who had turned five in August 1933. Another of Stephen's special duties was to regularly examine the police for venereal disease. That such a Papuan native, educated, in so high a position, and of so high a reputation should do anything wrong made his fall a great one; that he should be a member of the Headquarters staff of the Armed Native Constabulary made the fall terrible to Murray and others.

On 14 December 1933 the Prime Minister received a

telegram from H. W. Champion, who had been Acting Administrator since the middle of November when Murray had gone south. The telegram informed the Prime Minister, with regret, of a 'case of native indecently dealing with European girl aged five'. The native was Stephen Gorumbaru. The next day, Stephen appeared before the Magistrate's Court charged under sections 3 and 5 of the White Women's Protection Ordinance with rape and with unlawful carnal knowledge and his case was remanded until 19 December.

Two days later, the Executive Council met to consider 'papers relative to the defence of the native prisoner Gorumbaru (Stephen)' and —no doubt because of his high and trusted position in the Armed Native Constabulary—the council ordered that R. D. Bertie be asked to defend the accused. This was the first time that a man charged with a capital offence under the White Women's Protection Ordinance was to have the benefit of counsel.

'Owing to the illness of the child' on 19 December the Crown Law Officer asked for a further remand until 2 January and it was granted. The evidence which had already been revealed to the Acting Lieutenant-Governor was that the girl had been found to be suffering from gonorrhoea and that the Sergeant, who had admitted 'to one act of intercourse with her', said that he had had the disease for the previous two months but had concealed it.[11] The lack of documents is tantalising. How did the child's father discover next day that she had gonorrhoea?[12] What physical damage, if any, had been done? What did Stephen say in his confession? How was the confession made? What did the child say in her evidence? None of these crucial questions can be fully answered without the documents: one can only piece together bits of information from various sources.

After the remand, Stephen was sent back to gaol at Badili on 19 December to spend Christmas waiting for his trial; a miserable fate that was made even more miserable because, the gaoler reported, his offence had 'excited the anger and disgust of the 200 other prisoners who refused to have anything to do with [him]'. From this time on, whenever he was referred to by the newspapers, or by the Papuan government officials he was no longer 'Sergeant Gorumbaru'

123

or 'Stephen Gorumbaru' or 'Stephen' but 'Gorumbaru alias Stephen', an appellation with strong criminal overtones. As a trusted policeman he could be called by a European name, but when he became a criminal, he forfeited his right to a European name. All those Papuans I have spoken to recall the case today. They know—and knew—him as 'Stephen'.

While Stephen awaited his trial and his case was *sub judice* a long inflammatory article was published in *Smith's Weekly* under provocative headlines in huge type:

ALL MEN ARE BROTHERS—BUT ARE THEY?
PORT MORESBY HORROR
Terrible Indictment of Commonwealth Government
GROWING MENACE OF NATIVE ARROGANCE
Culmination of Long Series of Assaults on White Women and Children.[13]

The story was accompanied by a page-wide drawing depicting a bare-topped and lap-lapped Papuan crawling towards a verandah on which a small girl is playing with her dolls. The story began: 'There is a small white child—a girl—lying ill at Port Moresby, capital of the Territory of Papua. Not yet six years old, she is grievously wounded in body—and, as well is in the physicians hands. She is the victim of native outrage.' The article linked the reprieve of Miaro with this outrage, it tangled the case of Miaro and that of a murder suspect and, instead of attacking the Papuan Administration for the state of affairs, it concentrated all its considerable venom on the Commonwealth Government.

Recalling other cases of 'native arrogance' the writer quoted the Rabaul strike and the case of a Mrs Huson of Buka Island who had been molested by a native. 'I can stand a lot', Mrs Huson was quoted, 'but there is one thing I will not stand, and that is a nigger putting his hands on me, an Australian white woman.' These examples set the mood for a highly coloured account of Gorumbaru's actions, embroidered with circumstantial detail and told in violent, angry prose, 'The verandah was a place of comfortable shade. The scene, with the child so seriously engrossed in her game, was a perfect tropic idyll . . . The child was playing, as it were, in a region where ape-minds and human bodies roamed at large with not even fear any longer to hold them in leash.'

124

He 'dragged her into the room . . . This time it was no adult woman fighting with the tiger-cat fury of desperation, but a helpless almost babe, which [sic] was to know this black brute of the mission schools.' An influential resident of Port Moresby was quoted as saying that papers should 'make a hell of a noise' otherwise the Commonwealth Government would intervene again and let the native off. 'That black brute, who has been taught that in the eyes of God, he is the white man's brother, should, by his public death, teach the other natives that the doctrine is purely figurative and not actual.' The article bore all the marks of having been written with information supplied by James, probably by James himself.

James's paper did not make a hell of a noise. It had no need to. It made no noise at all and simply reported the case as it came up through the lower court and the Central Court with no details, calmly, with little sound and no fury. No citizens' opinions were presented in letters, no meetings were called, no motions urging anything. After the brouhaha which Miaro's reprieve had aroused, it must have been clear even to James that the Papuan Government was as one with the rest of Moresby white opinion, and only the Commonwealth Government might need stiffening. There was little doubt that the Commonwealth Government would have placed its Papuan Administration in an impossible position had it again intervened in a case involving such a universally horrifying offence committed by a trusted sergeant of police. The Labor government of Miaro's day had been replaced in January 1932 by the United Australia Party led by J. A. Lyons. But it is doubtful that even Scullin's government could have intervened successfully in this case.

On 2 January 1934 Gorumbaru was committed for trial to the Central Court and appeared there before Mr Justice Gore on 12 January on three charges under the White Women's Protection Ordinance:

That on the 12th day of December 1933, he did

1. Commit rape upon a European girl . . .
2. Have unlawful carnal knowledge of a European girl under 14 years . . .

3. Unlawfully and indecently deal with a European girl under 14 . . .

A plea of Not Guilty was entered for Stephen.

The trial began with a huge injustice and with a lie. As soon as the Crown Law Officer, E. B. Bignold, announced his appearance for the Crown, His Honour Mr Justice Gore asked if the accused was represented. Bignold replied that he was not, since R. D. Bertie, who had agreed when asked by the Executive Council to defend Stephen 'provided he was in the Territory when the matter came to trial', was 'unfortunately' out of the Territory, and though, Bignold added, he had 'understood' that he was to be back on 18 January, 'it now appeared' that he would not return until 8 February. His Honour believed that 'in the interests of justice' the trial should proceed, it being then over two months between the alleged offence and the trial of the defendant. So, in the interests of justice, Gorumbaru, alias Stephen, stood undefended.[15]

But this was not at all what Bertie had said. When the Acting Lieutenant-Governor and his Executive Council had ordered that Bertie be asked to defend Gorumbaru, a letter was sent to him on the same day, 16 December. Two days later Bertie had replied and accepted the brief, but in a postscript to his letter he added:

since writing the above, I have heard from Mr. Bignold that the case cannot be heard in the lower Court today, and will be adjourned for a week at least. I am leaving on the Macdhui on Wednesday, so will not be available in the lower Court. However, I can appear in the Central Court if he is committed.[16]

This, as A. P. Lyons later pointed out, was a very different statement of the case from that which Bignold had given (and which Judge Gore took down in his notes of the trial), that Bertie would defend 'if he was back'. Bertie's letter left no doubt about his being back and in fact Judge Gore had discovered from the manager of Burns Philp that he was booked on the *Montoro*, due in Port on 8 February.[17]

On the first day of the trial, the evidence came from the child, 'several other witnesses' and from the defendant's admission made on the day after the alleged offence to the Headquarters Officer, in front of other people.[18] After evidence had been taken, the accused made a statement and the Court adjourned until the following Monday, 15 January. On that day Judge Gore found Stephen guilty of the first and most serious charge of rape, for which, under the White Women's Protection Ordinance, there was only one sentence: death.

There is not much more evidence to be pieced together after the Central Court trial than after the Magistrate's Court except that a member of the Executive Council, A. P. Lyons, who had read the evidence, said that 'there was no appearance of ravishing in the occurrence' and that the child 'did not report the matter to either of her parents'.[19] Stephen went back to gaol after his sentence to wait for the Executive Council to confirm the court's decisions and to decide on the time and place of his death. The Council met on 18 January and this time Arthur Jewell was present, the first non-official member of the Executive Council sitting at his second meeting.

After considering the case, the Executive Council confirmed the death sentence on the vote of H. W. Champion, the Acting Lieutenant-Governor; for while the Official Secretary, H. L. Murray and Arthur Jewell voted for the death sentence, the Commissioner for Native Affairs and the Director of Public Works voted against it. These were the only members present at the meeting. The execution was fixed for the morning of Monday 29 January at Badili gaol.

J. T. O'Malley, Commissioner for Native Affairs, who voted against Stephen's death as he had voted against Miaro's, had had a long and responsible career in the Papuan public service and was a very close friend of Hubert Murray.[20] He dissented here on the sophisticated paternal grounds that 'in regard to sexual offences we should not attach the same standards of criminal responsibility to a native of Papua as we do to a European, because, in such cases, although we are dealing with human nature, it is human nature on a very different plane to our own'. He gave a clear and humane exposition of his view of Papuan sexuality and why it should be taken into account in this case. 'We are dealing with human nature of a primitive people, who, we know, have strong animal propensities, the environment and atmosphere of whose lives—like the lives of generations of their ancestors—is bound up in the matter of sex to such an extent that it absorbs all other interests and desires, so that gratification of their sexual impulses is such a usual and ordinary thing for them in their primitive life that it is impossible for their mentality to regard sexual offences with the seriousness that we do.'[21] O'Malley therefore believed that drastic penalties should not be exacted for these crimes. In time, he added, we would be justified in making Papuans bear the same standard of criminal responsibility as Europeans. As this, in fact, was the basis of the administration of law in Papua,[22] O'Malley's argument stood to reason; but in the case of Gorumbaru, in Port Moresby, reason was *hors de concours*.

O'Malley protested also on the ground that the trial had not been justly conducted. The court's decision not to adjourn the case had deprived Gorumbaru of defending counsel: this was an error in judgment for if the court feared that the child would forget her evidence, then it could have heard that evidence first and then adjourned the trial. If he had had a defending counsel, the accused would have had the benefit of cross-examination and it is quite possible that counsel could have shown extenuating circumstances.

A. P. Lyons also attacked the lack of defence, though he had objections of another order. Lyons, too, was an old hand in the Papuan service. A Queenslander, born in 1887, he had joined it in 1906, first as a clerk in the Government Secretary's department then moving into outside service. He had been Assistant Resident Magistrate of the Northern Division based at Kokoda and then Resident Magistrate in various stations: eight years at Daru, four years at Misima and six at Samarai. In 1930, he returned to Port Moresby as Director of Public Works and a member of the Executive Council. Lyons's objections were detailed carefully. First he gave the history of Gorumbaru's defence counsel and revealed the lie that had been told in the Central Court about Bertie's response to the request that he defend the accused.

His reasons for dissenting were first, that the accused was entitled to have his case adjourned for twenty-seven days until 8 February, the day on which the *Montoro*, with Bertie aboard, would dock. As it was, no prosecution witness had been cross-examined, the child had given her evidence without oath and was not questioned on anything else to test her memory. A defence lawyer might have put Stephen in the box or might have appealed to the High Court against his conviction. 'A person on trial for a Crime', Lyons wrote, 'and particularly for a crime of which the punishment is or is liable to be death, is entitled to the greatest consideration, so I am of the opinion that the trial judge erred in not adjourning the trial of [Gorumbaru].'

Lyons's second objection was that the evidence had established unlawful carnal knowledge rather than rape or attempted rape and that since under both the Criminal Code and the White Women's Protection Ordinance the penalty for unlawful carnal knowledge was life imprisonment, the death sentence was not just. On this point he was not legally sound, since though rape implies lack of consent and though there was no appearance of ravishing in the occurrence, lack of consent has been held to be immaterial in the case of girls so young as not to be in a position to decide whether to consent or to resist. In a girl as young as this it would certainly have been immaterial.[23] But Lyons was concerned that a man should not be hanged for a rape in which there had been no evidence of violence and where the child did not report the matter to either of her parents.

Lyons's final objection was to the Ordinance itself. The law in regard to rape was not free from duplicity, he suggested:

> if rape or attempted rape by a black man on a European woman or girl is to be regarded as deserving greater punishment than rape or attempted rape committed by a European on either a European woman or girl or a black or half-caste woman or girl, then the law should say so without ambiguity.

While theoretically, the provisions of the White Women's Protection Ordinance could apply equally to white men as black, he continued, it is universally believed by European residents of the Territory that they were framed to punish only black offenders. Our law ought to be untainted even with the suspicion that it is possible to use it, though subconsciously, to the prejudice of the black man. I do not think it is at present.

The law ought especially to be free from duplicity, said Lyons 'in a black man's country where, usually, the European atmosphere is highly charged with colour prejudice'.[24]

Even such eloquent protest was fruitless this time. In a covering letter sent to the Prime Minister, J. A. Lyons, with the two dissenting statements, Champion insisted that 'the accused had had a fair trial and that the trial was not prejudicially affected by the absence of counsel assigned for the defence'.[25] It was an extraordinary assertion. There was a united front of all sections of the white community before the horror of the crime, and amongst most on the necessity for the death sentence; the presence on the Executive Council of a non-official member cemented the unity between government and commerce, a unity reflected in the pages of the *Courier* and in the absence of any agitation.

'Kaloa' in the *Bulletin* reported that 'most white New Guinea residents will hope that the sentence of death passed by Judge Gore on a policeman for assaulting a European child less than five years old will be carried out'.[26] *Pacific Islands Monthly*'s correspondent reported Stephen's case and judged the responsibility for the occurrence to be not upon Papuan officials, but upon Australian politicians and 'namby-pamby sentimentalists' who had so often interfered between Papuan officials and the native delinquents whom it was their duty to punish. *Pacific Islands Monthly* did think that trying natives by British court procedure was ridiculous. The 'definite statement of the white adult that a native has committed an offence should be enough to convict that native'.[27]

From this period the opposition of white residents—particularly old hands—turned more and more against the Australian Government and, except for a short period after World War II when the Labor Government saddled them with Colonel J. K. Murray—whom they dubbed 'Kanaka Jack'—they have never again expressed that ferocity against the Papuan administration shown in the 1920s and 1930s.

The unanimity of the white population in the face of this example of the 'Black Peril' may have been further cemented by the economic crisis which the Territory was experiencing and by Murray's battle with the Australian Government for restoration of the Australian grant to its pre-depression size. Cursed, in W. C. Marr, with the worst Minister he had ever had,[28] Murray was not cursed this time with a petitioning group of residents ready to blame him for every attack on a white woman. He had a non-official member on his Executive Council and on this occasion, fortunately for himself, he was out of Papua for the whole of January, returning on the *Montoro* with R. D. Bertie, and then staying only for ten days before taking the same ship on its return voyage to attend an Administrators' conference. Nor was Murray cursed with Commonwealth intervention: there was no last minute reprieve.

While Gorumbaru was in prison waiting execution, he further disappointed his old patrons and teachers by turning from the Anglican faith to the Roman Catholic for the reason—or so it was said by Anglicans—that Father McEncroe told him he could ensure an acquittal.[29] A Roman Catholic view is different. 'He said he wanted to become a Catholic', wrote Hubert Murray to his son, 'so Fr. McEnroe [*sic*] received him . . . But Father Mac is very unpopular among a certain set (not of our holy Church) because they say the native should be allowed to go to Hell.'[30] Whatever intercessions may have been made, none was successful; and at eight o'clock of the morning of 29 January 1934, Gorumbaru alias Stephen went to his death.

The gallows had been erected on the lower part of the hill outside the gaol at Badili and Igo Erua, Port Moresby correspondent for the *Papuan Villager*, reported that a great number of people from the town and from all the villages came to see the execution; but it was not possible to see it, because the gallows were screened from view. According to Stephen Ame's recollection, hundreds and hundreds of people saw him hanged, although a fence had been erected. They stood on the hills overlooking the gaol. Percy Chatterton estimates that four or five hundred Papuans walked to Badili, including *all* the pupils from his school at Hanuabada. The *Sydney Morning Herald* reported that about five hundred were there, but the *Courier* estimated over two thousand. James so much approved the execution that perhaps he exaggerated the number of Papuans who were there to benefit from its lesson.

It is not certain how many of those to whom his execution was intended to be an awful warning actually saw Stephen die his 'very brave death'.[31] Those who certainly did were W. E. Giblin, the doctor; W. J. Lambden, the Acting Sheriff; J. H. Sutton, the gaoler; T. P. Gough, the European constable and M. McEncroe, M.S.C., the priest in the presence of whom he was hanged by the neck until he was dead. His demeanour, the *Papuan Courier* reported, had been perfectly calm; and in a last statement 'he asked that a message be sent to the parents of the child expressing sorrow for the wrong he had done them'.

On the day of the execution, the Acting Lieutenant-Governor, the Official Secretary, Mr Justice Gore and the Crown Law Officer all embarked on the *Laurabada* and left Port Moresby for an official visit to Samarai. Eleven days after Stephen had been hanged, R. D. Bertie returned to Port—as he had said he would—after spending a short holiday in Australia.

Sir Hubert Murray wrote of the case in his *Annual Report* that it had been 'a terrible case'; but he washed his hands of all responsibility for it in terms which, though familiar in the Papuan public service, were unworthy of him: 'The accused made no attempt to deny the charge, the evidence of which, I am told, was conclusive. I say "I am told" because I was away on leave at the time and have no personal knowledge of the case.' He praised the courage and resolution of Gorumbaru on his death as the 'sole redeeming feature of the whole revolting tragedy' and made this judgment: 'Bitter disappointment seems to be the inevitable lot of all who take an interest in the progress of the native race, and the disappointment is not lessened by the chorus of "I told you so" that rises on all hands when some wretched native commits an unusually abominable offence.'

Bitter disappointment is evident in Murray's obituary

for Sergeant Major Simoi, whose death was reported in the same *Annual Report* as Stephen's execution and alongside another disaster—the conviction for murder of two members of the Armed Native Constabulary—which must have made him despair of much of his work. Simoi, said Murray, was a man of strong character and marked personality, gifts 'not commonly found among natives of this Territory'.[32] It was a bitter year in other ways for Murray; in June 1934, Lady Murray left Papua for good.

Stephen Gorumbaru's death was a result of all the bitter, fearful and angry emotions which white residents felt for the natives of the place where they lived, of their ambivalence towards Sir Hubert Murray, and opposition to the metropolitan government and of their own pride in purity of race. His death was an object lesson to all Papuans.

After his death, defects in the existing laws were discerned and harsher penalties for already existing crimes were again demanded by the residents, as if they were unconvinced that even hanging would be enough of a deterrent. In July 1934 the Government Secretary introduced into the Legislative Council an Ordinance to amend the White Women's Protection Ordinance. Under the original Ordinance, if the evidence against a person accused of rape would not support a conviction, the only alternative verdicts open to the court (if the evidence was sufficient) were conviction for attempted rape or unlawful and indecent assault, or the person could be convicted under the Criminal Code in which penalties were much lighter. The amending Ordinance provided more alternatives. It added to section 7 of the original Ordinance provisions that a person indicted for rape, if not convicted of rape, might be convicted of the original alternative plus having or attempting to have unlawful carnal knowledge of a European girl, or unlawfully and indecently dealing with a European girl. The amending Ordinance also made the White Women's Protection Ordinance exclusive for these offences by adding the following proviso: 'Provided that where an offence is punishable under the *Criminal Code* and also under this Ordinance the accused person shall be charged with the offence punishable under this Ordinance, and not with that punishable under the *Criminal Code.*'

The Executive wanted the same powers under the White Women's Protection Ordinance as it had under the code of convicting for alternate offences where they had been proved by the evidence, although the original charge may have been a different one; it also wanted to 'remove any doubt that the White Women's Protection Ordinance supersedes the Criminal Code as far as white women are concerned'.[33]

During the debate on the Bill, Arthur Jewell put forward further amendments. He wanted proper punishment provided for a native or anybody found unlawfully in the sleeping apartment of any European woman or girl. As things stood, the code provided a penalty of one year in prison with hard labour for anyone entering a house, yard or curtilage with the intent indecently to annoy any female inmate; the White Women's Protection Ordinance defined a crime called indecent assault—the one that had been used to convict men who touched a sleeping white woman—for which the punishment was imprisonment for life. Jewell's contention was that, since every native who was in a white woman's sleeping apartment had the intention of committing an indecent assault, even though he may have been prevented from carrying it out, a punishment of one year in prison was quite inadequate. 'To my mind', he said, 'it is the intent that constitutes the crime in this case, and, not only that, the mental effect upon the woman is just the same whether she is touched or not.' The official members objected to this position on the grounds that there might be legitimate grounds for entering the apartment—to collect a box of matches, for example—and that intent ought not to be presumed but proved. Jewell insisted that the mere fact of a native being found in the apartment was sufficient to establish intent, whereupon A. P. Lyons reminded him that the White Women's Protection Ordinance was not meant for natives only, a fiction which did not move Arthur Jewell. He came to the committee stage of debate with a motion which provided that evidence of the presence of a person 'at any time between the hours of 10 p.m. and 5 a.m. in the bedroom in which there is a European female may be taken as prima facie evidence of an intent indecently to annoy and insult her'.[34]

After some severe criticism by official members, and opposition from John Gusth Nelsson, a non-official member, and after Murray made one of his rare interventions in debate to explain how hard it was in law to prove intent, Arthur Jewell withdrew his amendment. When the Bill was passed and assented to, 'Onlooker' sneered in the *Courier*:

Each succeeding year leaves the onlooker more in doubt as to the reason for the existence of the unofficial members on the Legislative Council of Papua . . . The suggestion that a boy might go into his mistress's bedroom at 5 o'clock in the morning to get a box of matches . . . did credit to his imagination, gave too much for the energy of the native, and the reverse to any European woman who could be so lax as to make such an action necessary.

Six   The Hanging in History and Fiction

STEPHEN'S hanging, the first under the White Women's Protection Ordinance, was a tremendous event in the town.[1] Every Papuan who lived in or near Port Moresby at the time remembers the hanging vividly and those who were too young have had the story told to them by their elders. The *Papuan Villager*'s Port Moresby correspondent, Igo Erua, told a brief, unembellished and true story in his column: A Native named Gorumbaru (Stephen) formerly a Sergeant of Armed Constabulary at Port Moresby, was hanged at the Port Moresby Gaol on 29th ultimo at 8 o'clock in the morning. He had been convicted for doing a bad thing to a little white girl.

The very fact of his hanging and the manner of his trial however stuck in the gullets of many of the white residents at the time and jammed their memories of events. They could not talk truthfully about it at the time and their later recollections of the case are almost all false. H. W. Champion, who had given the casting vote for Stephen's execution in 1934, remembered the case in 1970 as 'the only action taken under the Ordinance' and he believed that it happened 'well after Sir Hubert Murray's death'. He recalled that Gorumbaru from the scaffold 'warned the assembled natives against interfering with European females'[2] but if such a warning had been issued it is incredible that it was not reported at the time. His son, Ivan Champion, recalling the event also in 1970, said that the hanging 'had a sobering effect on the natives generally' and that 'it was a long time before any other sex offence took place'.[3]

This was what the white residents most fondly believed, perhaps, but it was not so. The first case was heard in the Central Court not two months after Stephen was hanged, the second in May 1934, and a third in June 1934. These were all cases of entering with intent and those convicted received relatively minor sentences. On 20 June 1934, five months after the hanging, a Rossel Island man was charged under section 4 of the White Women's Protection Ordinance and convicted of indecent assault of a European female. He was sentenced to ten years' imprisonment with hard labour.[4]

It is not only later recollections which are faulty. The *Sydney Morning Herald*'s Port Moresby correspondent on 17 January 1934 told his readers about the hanging and mentioned the trial which had preceded it: 'Every effort was made to persuade the accused to have legal assistance, but he considered himself capable of managing his own case.' The Melbourne *Argus* on the same day told its readers that 'the accused refused legal counsel and managed his own case'. These reports must have been sent to the southern papers by a Port Moresby correspondent who, even if he did not know the inside story of the discussion in the Executive Council about Stephen's defence, and even if he had not been in the Central Court and heard the argument, must either have invented the lie of Stephen's refusal of a defence counsel or innocently repeated the lie to his readers.

Four years after the trial, in August 1938, *Pacific Islands Monthly* published an account from its Port Moresby correspondent Mollie Lett, of the death sentence passed on Karo—who had been one of the witnesses in Miaro's trial—for the murder of a warder, his wife and small daughter at Badili gaol. When Karo was executed, the correspondent wrote, it would be the fifth occasion on which a native had been executed in the Territory. The correspondent listed the executions:

1893	for the murder of a member of the A.N.C.
1913-14	for the murder of two carriers
1914-15	for the murder of a member of the A.N.C.
1915-16	for murder

The execution of January 1934 is missing.[5] Judge Gore did not mention the case of Stephen in his book of reminiscences, *Justice versus Sorcery*; nor did Lewis Lett in his biography of Hubert Murray. In 1969 when the Crown Solicitor of the Territory of Papua and New Guinea referred to the White Women's Protection Ordinance in a discussion of New Guinea law, he said of it that 'it was given wide publicity, the [rape] statistics returned to normal, and *no one was hanged*'.[6]

It seems that no one can bear to tell the truth about the Ordinance. We have already seen above how untrue Lewis Lett's account of it is. Ian Stuart, in his book *Port Moresby Yesterday and Today*, writes of the White Women's Protection Ordinance only that under its provisions 'it was an offence for a Papuan to be within the town area without permission after nine o'clock at night',[7] which is not the case, since the Ordinance contained no curfew provisions; these had their origins in the much earlier Native Labour Regulations.[8]

The most realistic account of life in pre-war Port Moresby, in which the author attempts to show the importance of the White Women's Protection Ordinance and explain it by describing and analysing the atmosphere among the white residents, and the only account at all of the hanging, appears in fictional form. The story of Stephen Gorumbaru as a paradigm of the colonial condition in Papua and particularly in Port Moresby stuck in the mind and heart of a member of the Papuan public service. Gilbert Munro Turnbull, who had been employed as an architect in the Department of Public Works at the time of Stephen's death and had been Acting Director of Public Works during Lyons's absence on leave, resigned from the service on superannuation at the end of that year.

Turnbull had arrived in Papua in 1913, aged twenty-three, after practising as an architect in the United States, Canada and Mexico. He began trading and planting in the Eastern Division. In 1914 he joined the public service as a member of the Lands Department and then became architect to the Department of Works in Port Moresby, where he designed the Treasury building, the European hospital, the government stores and the Roman Catholic presbytery. He had another life as a writer, and published three novels and many short stories—all on Papuan themes—before he died of pneumonia in his forty-ninth year at Bellingen on the north coast of New South Wales. He had been spending the winter there and working on a new novel. This novel, *Portrait of a Savage*, was Turnbull's recollection, in Bellingen's tranquility, of life in Port Moresby during the 1920s and 1930s; in particular of the relations between black and white and the panic which produced the White Woman's Protection Ordinance and the death of Stephen.[9]

Set mainly in Port Moresby in the period from World War I until 1934, the novel rings with the truth of its events and displays a keen observation of events and characters. The theme is the degradation of a young Papuan, Mark-Bopumu, a degradation which was thorough and the result of many factors: mission training which had cut off his traditional roots; work as a houseboy in Port Moresby which gave him lowly work under an intolerant and weak white master and put him in the path of gamblers, drunkards and the no-good wife of a shady European trader. The plot covers his whole life from the days with the mission, where he became intimate with a white boy of his own age, and follows him from the mission in the Eastern Division to Moresby.

Turnbull makes explicit in fiction what Murray, Lett and Bensted had hinted at in their accusations against white women. In an early chapter he gives an example of irresponsible behaviour by white women. The Hon. William Colvin, D.S.O., M.C., an important government official, member of the Executive Council with a high, though unspecified position and all the marks of a departmental head, is driving along Ela Beach Road in the company of Ingram, a young and weak public servant. As they pass a labour compound, they hear the sounds of a gramophone with boisterous uproar as accompaniment, and see natives flocking towards the sound. They stop to investigate the uproar which turns out to be a performance by two strapping men from the Western Division who are giving a parody of a one-step. The 'woman' wore 'a pair of lacy bloomers that had once been dainty; pink corsets were lashed around his waist, the broken suspenders being tied to soiled silk stockings that wrinkled around his bulging calves'. His face was powdered with flour, and an empty bottle hung from his wrist, as though a vanity bag. The record finished, the 'woman' reclined on a packing case and with legs outthrust called, mincingly, 'Boy! Come here, my boy. You pull'm off stockings, my boy.' Colvin strides in, breaks up the performance, orders the actors to take off the clothes and burn them, to report to the R.M.'s office in the morning, to go back to their villages and stay there and never again come to 'a white man's town'.

Colvin and the young officer embody the two white male attitudes we have already seen; Ingram is for beating up the performers for their travesty of white womanhood but Colvin calms him. 'There are white women who get half sozzled in public aren't there?' he asserts. There 'may be some who order their houseboys to take off their stockings for all I know'. In either case, the play-acting itself was seen as a danger to white prestige.

This play-acting was clearly an important way in which Papuans could assimilate and comment on the strange ways of the white men; legitimate versions of it were put on by missions, and Murray commented on the excellent imitations of white men which formed part of a performance arranged for him at the Fyfe Bay L.M.S. station.[10] Illegal performances, similar to the one described by Turnbull, in which Papuans parodied or acted straight dramas of white behaviour were recorded by J. E. Nixonwestwood[11] and in the evidence against Oelrichs, Resident Magistrate of the North Eastern Division, in 1913. Several men were arrested in the Eroro area for 'playing long moonlight olosem government' which in Papuan pidgin meant taking the part of government officials and acting their behaviour.[12] It mattered not whether the performance was straight; any attempt by Papuans to imitate white men was necessarily a parody in the eyes of its objects.

Turnbull's novel also catches the mood of the town after the case of 'Rex versus Ganimura', a Papuan Peeping Tom whose actions bring about the passage of the White Woman's Protection Ordinance and cause the newspaper *The Papuan Planter* to warn the government that Judge Lynch makes no fuss about justice, and that from his court there is no appeal'.

The climax of the plot is the arrest in Port Moresby of the mission-educated and handsome young Mark-Bopumu after a rebellious and confused early career. One night he creeps into the bedroom of the shady trader with whom his public service employer is entangled in order to steal a pack of cards and is confronted by the trader's half-drunken wife, sprawled on her bed, waiting for her lover. 'She looked at Mark with an expression in her eyes that had stirred and excited him many times, an expression that should not have been in the eyes of a Sinabada', and urgently began to seduce him. She had almost succeeded, when her lover appeared and she had the presence of mind to scream 'Rape' which, as she knew Mark well, meant his certain arrest.

The reaction of the Port Moresby residents is well described by Turnbull and analysed thus: 'A sudden crashing shock had descended upon the township. Something that was white pride, white honour, had been hurled down, befouled, and trampled on by beasts.' Lynching is in the air. Some citizens hate the idea of a trial where a 'white woman suffers horribly in the witness box with a nigger facing her in the dock' but Mark does come to trial with his defence, which is the true story of what happened to him that night, a story the reader has already heard as it happened. But the defence is 'so fantastic' that it is quite impossible for Judge Loring to accept it, though the more realistic and sympathetic characters in the novel know his conclusion to be 'silly twaddle'.

Turnbull was not prepared to incorporate Murray or Judge Gore into his fiction; nor does he make any judgment of their part in the tragedy. Murray certainly would not have thought the tale of seduction fantastic, since he believed, as Colvin in the novel believed, that there were women whose servants performed intimate and therefore dangerous services for them. In Colvin and Loring he shows two white male positions: one which blamed women for the attacks on themselves, the other which blamed their attackers. He put his own thoughts into the mouth of Tony Gale, a young white man who has known Mark as a boy on the mission. Addressing all white residents of Papua—including himself —Tony Gale muses bitterly:

> When a white man fell foul of the law for molesting a native girl, nine times out of ten you sniggered. You didn't snigger when the boot was on the other foot. Your point of view changed completely. The code! That racial honour that requires arrogance, aggression, violence for its defence; that greatest of all obsessions, the obsession of racial superiority.

Colvin can see what is wrong. He is a portrait based perhaps on A. P. Lyons, Turnbull's Director, whose position Turnbull filled while Lyons was on leave in 1934 after the hanging and from whom he must have heard serious objections to the whole case of Stephen Gorumbaru. Colvin knew that Mark was innocent of the crime for which he was convicted, but he also knew that if the Executive Council were to commute the death sentence the white population would bring the Administration down. He wondered whether he ought to resign in protest and decided that it would be a useless gesture as in all likelihood a worse man than himself would take his place. Mark-Bopumu was hanged and Colvin continued in his job.

Given the loss of all pre-war court records except the Register of Criminal Cases, given the inaccuracy of the historians, the conspiracy of silence about the facts of the White Women's Protection Ordinance, and the perversions of memory in the survivors, such a portrait as Turnbull provides of those years throws invaluable light on Port Moresby's pre-war life. Together with the recollections of Papuans who worked and lived there it may give us something like an accurate account; though it will probably never be possible to discover how many of the cases of assault brought before the courts were genuine sexual assaults, how many were the result of fear and fevered imagination which interpreted every Papuan movement towards a white woman as a sexual assault—at least in intent—and how many, if any, were liaisons repudiated by the women in a moment of panic and fear of discovery. It is safe to say about the cases which became public and about which we have information through Papuan administration archives that none were of this last sort.

Without evidence, white people have taken their pick of two connected explanations for whatever number of sexual assaults they care to acknowledge; that all natives are animals who will rape anyone if they need sexual relief or are excited; and that women are themselves the cause of their own attack by exciting men, perhaps unwittingly, and that they were more to blame than the men because they should have known better. The men were savages who could not have been expected to act differently. The explanation given by those Papuan men who lived in Port Moresby before the war, or who have heard about it from their elders, is not surprisingly the second one; and it is revealing of the deeply mysterious and fearful world of sex and race that though Papuan men and European men might have feared and hated each other cordially and though they shared no other myths, they had in common the myth of the white lady and the towel.

Epilogue

THE White Women's Protection Ordinance has gone. It and other parts of the criminal law were hurriedly repealed by the Legislative Council in 1958 after the Minister for Territories had directed that all discriminatory legislation be repealed.[1] The Secretary for Law, W. W. Watkins, when introducing the amendments in the Legislative Council, gave reasons for the change which were as lacking in candour as those which had been put forward by the Lieutenant-Governor when he had introduced the Bill in 1926.

Firstly, said Watkins, there were 'conflicting laws in the Territory'. Secondly, 'to impose the death penalty for rape is an invitation to the rapist to kill his victim and thus dispose of the evidence', so the government proposed to 'follow the normal practice elsewhere' of making life imprisonment the penalty for rape. 'That highly discriminatory piece of legislation the White Women's Protection Ordinance of Papua' was therefore to be repealed. Watkins did not mention that the Australian Government had ordered the repeal nor that it was responding to United Nations pressure, just as Murray had not explained why the white residents' pressure which he had declared hysterical and dangerously wrong-headed in August had been given in to in January, that the death penalty for *attempted* rape was the real nub of the Ordinance.

The fact that the laws of the whole Territory of Papua and New Guinea were not consistent on rape was an historical accident: the white residents of Rabaul in 1936 had agitated for the provision of a similar Ordinance but their campaign was suspended after the eruption of Vulcan on 29 May 1937. When they resumed agitation in August 1937, a Bill for an Ordinance Relating to Offences against European Women was prepared—with provisions identical with those of the White Women's Protection Ordinance—but then suddenly abandoned. Instead the Criminal Code was amended, providing heavier penalties for sexual crimes, but there was no death penalty for attempted rape, the death penalty for rape was included but made optional not obligatory upon the judge, and, as throughout the Criminal Code, there was no discrimination as to the race of the victim. Why this was done cannot be explained with certainty for the relevant papers in the file on the proposed Ordinance in the Commonwealth Archives Office have been enclosed in brown manila envelopes and scholars are not permitted to read them. I suspect it was an Australian Cabinet decision anticipating League of Nations opposition; when I was working on the material in 1971, all Cabinet papers were closed to access by research workers. The inconsistencies in the laws of the Territory remained after the repeal of the Ordinance, leaving a great variety of differences in regard to ages and penalties in sex offences on young females, differences remaining to the present day. The reasons for the repeal were other than those W. W. Watkins had offered in the Legislative Council; as Sir Hubert Murray's reasons for his introduction of the Ordinance had been.

After W. W. Watkins had made his statement of explanation, E. A. James and other non-official members of the Legislative Council complained that they had not had time to study the Bills. 'I cannot for the life of me see,' said James, 'why after 30 or 40 years it was necessary that these amendments should go through after about seven days' notice.' But he did not speak against the Bills. Only B. E. Fairfax-Ross, non-official member, reminded those who now talked of discrimination that they 'must not forget that where it does exist it was specifically planned to exist by thoughtful and benign Administrators of this country in the past'. And he continued in much the same words as Hubert Murray had used when defending the Ordinance: 'Discrimination in law, Sir, often seems to me to be very necessary in dealing with two groups of people in very different stages of development and with very different reactions to law and punishment and discrimination is not necessarily all bad.' Fairfax-Ross was speaking for many white residents, though none supported him in the Legislative Council, and the Bills passed through all stages in the time it took to read them, without amendment or debate.

The specific conditions which caused the Ordinance to be introduced have gone; the basic fear which lay beneath it remains. A fear of black sexual attack is still in the air of Port Moresby. The white newcomer soon learns of it. In *A Guide to Newcomers to Papua New Guinea* first published in 1957 by the Country Women's Association the following warning appears:

> Parents of little girls especially should not allow a familiar attitude to grow between a domestic servant and their children, but to bear in mind that the people of this country do not have the same social background or training as ourselves. Do not let your children run around unclothed. Make sure they always wear trunks or swim suits at least. There have been cases where children and women have been molested. A lot of people have the idea 'it cannot happen to me' but don't be too sure! It is your duty to guard against your child being injured, and prevent anyone from an act which he may regret later . . .
>
> In the home, on the streets, and even in the field of sport and swimming, bear in mind the phrase 'revealing clothing leads to provocation'. Do not appear before your staff in night attire or under-clothes.

The story of the lady with the towel is still told in Port Moresby. The suggestion is still current that women who are sexually assaulted have themselves to blame. In 1969 the fact that a young white woman was living with a black man was given as part explanation, part extenuation, for the attempt of another black man to rape her. Gossip exaggerates the number and seriousness of assaults, and today, as in the 1920s and 1930s, a sexual attack by a black man on a white woman is seen not as an individual case but as the early sign of a trend. There also remains in the town a fear by black men of accidental contact with white women. Older Papuans in particular step aside when a white woman comes towards them in the street, or the shop or the office; there is less physical contact between black and white people than is normal in cities or crowded areas; if a black man bumps into a white woman at Koke his apologies are likely to be effuse.

What has changed is the language in which the fears are couched. The warning of the Country Women's Association sounds very different from the *Papuan Courier*'s hysteria. These are women talking to women and warning them calmly of dangers; not enemies of a Lieutenant-Governor using an issue to discomfort or dislodge him. Changed too, among a significant number of people, is that concern with race purity and prestige which made any sexual relations between black and white so horrifying. White men marry black women and, sign of greater change, white women marry black men and this no longer causes the anger it did when the first white woman married a black man in Port Moresby in 1961. And changed radically, as a result, are the penalties and the discrimination as to the victim of sexual assault. A black man in 1971 who 'behaved indecently' towards a European girl aged seven pleaded guilty, was convicted, and received five months' gaol, although the Resident Magistrate thought he should have received nine months' gaol 'because the charge was a serious one'. Thirty years before he may well have been imprisoned for life, if not hanged.

That Sir Hubert Murray, a thoughtful and benign Administrator, passed the White Women's Protection Ordinance needs to be explained and not glossed over as it has been. Murray brought in the Bill, as he brought in all those regulations passed since 1908 in Papua whose purpose was to keep Papuans in an inferior position and to keep them apart from whites in the town, partly because he shared many of the assumptions of the white residents about black sexuality and inferiority and about the importance of white prestige in a colonial situation. Although he opposed the white residents on many important issues, in this case he bowed before the strong and concerted pressure of the most influential men in the town, those who had tried to engineer his dismissal a few years earlier. In doing so he added to the burden of inferiority which the colonial relationship had placed on the Papuans and to the injustices they had to bear in the white man's town.

NOTES *

Preface

1. In common with all who write about Papua or New Guinea, I do not know what to call the inhabitants. At the time of which I write, they were called 'natives' not in the sense of the indigenous inhabitants of some country, but in the sense that Miss Tox in *Dombey and Son* used it, of dark men unconnected 'with any geographical idea whatever'. I sometimes call the inhabitants natives, sometimes Papuans, sometimes by names given to various groups, for example Motu, or to various administrative divisions, for example Gulf.

2. 'The Pattern of Race Relations in Nineteenth Century Port Towns', *Journal of Pacific History*, Vol. 6, 1971, p. 45.

3. Philip Mason, *Patterns of Dominance*, London, 1970, p. 95.

4. See Francis West, *Hubert Murray*, Melbourne, 1968, especially Chapter VII, 'Public and private war'.

Chapter 1

1. *Some Experiences of a New Guinea Resident Magistrate*, London, 1921, p. 139.

2. Description of Port Moresby and Neighbourhood, ML, p. 45.

3. *Papuan Villager*, Vol. 2, No. 10, 15 October 1930, p. 6.

4. Ibid., Vol. 1, No. 10, 15 November 1929. 'Lagani-Namo'—'Good year' in the Motu language—was the pseudonym of R. A. Goodyear, a Port Moresby trade store owner.

5. For the origin of these ideas see Christine Bolt, *Victorian Attitudes to Race*, London, 1971.

6. *An Outpost in Papua*, London, 1911, p. 230.

7. Secretary to Administrator Barton, evidence before Royal Commission, para. 193.

8. Edith Turner, *Among Papuan Women*, Westminster, 1920, p. 5.

9. Chignell, *Outpost in Papua*, p. 230.

10. To Dr J. A. Blayney, Resident Magistrate of Central Division, 14 July 1898, LMS Letters. Also Lawes to Atlee Hunt, 4 September 1905, complaining that Captain Barton had organised a great carnival of dancing, thus undermining the mission's work.

11. *Papuan Villager*, Vol. 2, No. 4, 15 April 1930, p. 1.

12. Ibid., Vol. 1, No. 8, 16 September 1929, p. 3.

13. Quoted in Russell W. Abel, *Charles W. Abel of Kwato*, New York, 1934, pp. 50-1.

14. Territory of Papua, *Annual Report 1937-38*, p. 20.

15. See the clash between Hubert Murray and G. H. Pitt-Rivers in *Man*, 27 April 1929, 8 February 1931 on this last point.

* Abbreviations used are: CAO Commonwealth Archives Office; ML Mitchell Library, Sydney; NA National Archives of Papua New Guinea; NL National Library of Australia; *PD* Commonwealth of Australia, *Parliamentary Debates; PP* Commonwealth of Australia, *Parliamentary Papers.*

Chapter 1—Cont'd

16. *Papuan Villager*, Vol. 3, No. 1, 15 January 1931, p. 3.
17. 'Native Education', p. 49, Appendix to Sir Hubert Murray, *Native Administration in Papua*, June 1929.
18. J. H. P. Murray, introduction to J. G. Hides, *Through Wildest Papua*, London, 1935, p. 8.
19. *Papuan Villager*, Vol. 4, No. 1, January 1932, p. 1.
20. Ibid., Vol. 6, No. 11, 21 November 1934, p. 8. *Sinabada* is a Motu word, meaning big mother, and used of white women.
21. Stephen Ame recalls Sergeant Bagita as being the one who carried out this regulation.
22. *Papuan Villager*, Vol. 5, No. 5, 15 May 1933, p. 33.
23. *In the Land of Dohori*, Sydney, 1929, p. 208.
24. *The Blending of Cultures: an Essay in the Aims of Native Education*, Port Moresby, 1935, p. 6.
25. Union of South Africa, *Report of the Commission . . .* , p. 21.
26. *Outpost in Papua*, pp. 226-7.
27. *Discoveries and Surveys in New Guinea*, London, 1876, p. 139.
28. 'Notes on New Guinea and Its Inbabitants', *Journal of the Royal Geographical Society*, October 1880, p. 606.
29. James Chalmers and Wyatt Gill, *Work and Adventure in New Guinea 1877 to 1885*, London, 1885, p. 261.
30. Ibid., p. 265.
31. *Papua or British New Guinea*, London, 1912, p. 156.
32. Monckton, *Some Experiences*, p. 155.
33. 'Bouragi', *The Bulletin*, 30 December 1926. Bouragi was. a frequent correspondent in 1925 and 1926 on Papuan affairs.
34. Three examples, the Bishop of North Queensland, J. O. Feetham, praising Papuans in 1917, talks of 'black and ghoulish past traditions' (*From Samarai to Ambasi*, Sydney, 1917, p. 44); the Reverend J. P. Bodger, Anglican missionary in the North Eastern Division in a pamphlet praising the 'Fuzzy Wuzzy Angels' quotes the poem which includes this line 'and we're glad to call you friends in the time that is so black' (*Fuzzy Wuzzy Angels*, Sydney, 1944, p. 2); the Reverend J. B. Clark (LMS), obituary on Maulu Gaudi, pastor at Vabukori, 'he was white in every thing but his skin' (*Courier*, 30 October 1925). The first two are pamphlets in the Gill Collection in the Mitchell Library.
35. *The Bulletin*, 18 February 1926, p. 12.
36. Hubert Murray, Diary, Vol. 3, 20 February 1915, A3138-42, ML.
37. Hubert Murray, Letter to his sister-in-law, Lady Mary Murray, Gilbert's wife, 5 May 1926, Francis West, *Selected Letters of Hubert Murray*, Melbourne, 1970, p. 119.
38. Pp. 22, 20.
39. *Sands of Oro*, London, 1924, p. 274.
40. Beatrice Grimshaw, *White Savage Simon*, Sydney, 1919, pp. 23, 196.
41. Jack McLaren, *The Oil Seekers*, Sydney, 1921, p. 11.
42. *Isles of Adventure*, London, 1930, p. 29.
43. *The Oil Seekers*, p. 55.
44. *Feathers of Heaven*, Sydney, 1921, p. 55.
45. West, *Hubert Murray*, p. 89.
46. All cases in CAO:CRS G82, Items 1 and 2.

47. Pers. comm. from the late H. W. Champion, 7 May 1970.
48. Evidence of J. H. P. Murray before Royal Commission, 1906, para. 2061.
49. 24 March 1920, CAO:CRS G82, Item 3.
50. *The Bulletin*, 25 March 1926.
51. Ibid., 8 July 1926.
52. H. L. Griffin, *An Official in British New Guinea*, London, 1925, pp. 143-4. Griffin was acting against the law in sending the offenders to gaol. He ought to have whipped them himself, or had someone whip them in front of him.
53. CAO:CRS G69, Item 16/31.
54. *Two Roads of Papua*, London, 1935, p. 19. 'Momkeni' in *Pacific Islands Monthly*, July 1932, p. 17, describes the same behaviour in other women.
55. C. A. W. Monckton, *Last Days in New Guinea*, London, 1922, pp. 109-10.
56. Pers. comm. from the Reverend Percy Chatterton, 4 October 1971. Mr Chatterton said he would never preach again if the Papuans were not permitted to use the church and Mr McDonald left the church.
57. Murray to his daughter Mary Pinney, 11 May 1933, in West, *Letters*, p. 156. For an account of the whole Medical Assistants' episode and the resentment it aroused among white residents, see H. N. Nelson, 'Brown Doctors: White Prejudice', *New Guinea*, Vol. 5, No. 2, June-July 1970, pp. 21-8.
58. 10 September 1928, Patrol Reports, CAO:CRS G91.
59. *The Bulletin*, 15 November 1926.

Chapter 2

1. For a history of their settlement and a description of their work, see Peter Biskup, 'Foreign Coloured Labour in German New Guinea', *Journal of Pacific History*, Vol. 5, 1970, pp. 85-107.
2. Pers. comm. from Canon Ian Stuart, 12 October 1971. This could well have been the case in Rabaul. The Roman Catholic parish of Port Moresby has no records from which numbers of pupils at the school could have been obtained.
3. Letter, 21 March 1908, Atlee Hunt papers, MS 52, NL.
4. Lewis Lett, *Sir Hubert Murray of Papua*, Sydney, 1949, p. 219.
5. Population figures published in the *Annual Reports* for the years 1924-30 show arrivals, departures, births and deaths of the European population, divided into adult males and females and child males and females. During these years the adult female European population of Papua had risen by 156, the adult male by 115. The number of male children had risen by seventy-five and that of female children by ninety-three.
6. 'Ela', *The Bulletin*, 19 March 1930.
7. Nigel Oram, pers. comm.
8. Quoted in P. S. Allen, *Stewart's Handbook of the Pacific Islands*, Sydney, 1923, p. 325.
9. S. M. Lambert, *A Doctor in Paradise*, Melbourne, 1942, p. 16.
10. Mary Hall, *A Woman in the Antipodes*, London, 1914, p. 220.
11. *Papuan Courier*, 2 January 1925.
12. Lambert, *Doctor in Paradise*, p. 19. Among those he named were Loudon, Sefton and Jewell.

Chapter 2—Cont'd

13. Planters' Association of Papua, *Conditions in Papua*, Sydney, 1921, p. 6.
14. *Report by H. E. the Lieutenant-Governor of Papua to the Honourable Minister for Home and Territories on an article on 'Three Power Rule in New Guinea' by Mr. Rinzo Gond*, P.P. 1917-18-19, Vol. VI, p. 1628.
15. *Papuan Courier*, 5 March 1920.
16. Ibid., 19 March 1920.
17. Ibid., 8 October 1920. The *Courier* published the telegram part of a letter from 'Dinkum Aussie' who reported it as a rumour he had heard.
18. His Excellency to the Minister of State for Home and Territories, 16 October 1920, Report from H. E. Greenland (a public servant who was at the meeting), CAO:CRS G75, Item 22.
19. 10 November, 13 November, 26 December 1920, 6 January 25 January, 9 February 1921, CAO:CRS G76, Item 22.
20. Statement of Chief Postmaster to His Excellency, 18 February 1921 and Herbert to Minister of State for Home and Territories, 28 February 1921, CAO:CRS G82, Item 3.
21. West, *Letters*, p. 115.
22. Territory of Papua, *Annual Report 1925-26*, para. 501.
23. Ibid., *Annual Report 1920-21*, p. 9.
24. Octavius Stone, *A Few Months in New Guinea*, London, 1880, p. 193.
25. Jack Hides, *Savages in Serge*, London, 1938, p. 138.
26. Vincent Eri, *The Crocodile*, Brisbane, 1970, p. 24.
27. *Papuan Courier*, 2 January 1925.
28. 'Blue Hum', letter to ibid., 30 April 1926.
29. Territory of Papua, *Government Gazette*, Vol. IX, No. 2, 4 February 1914.
30. *Papuan Courier*, 17 September 1920.
31. C. G. Seligman, *The Melanesians of British New Guinea*, Cambridge, 1910, p. 135.
32. Testimony of Stephen Ame of Beipa'a village, near Bereina, Central District.
33. Testimony of Stephen Ame of Beipa'a and of Varuko Morea of Porebada, a village near Port Moresby.
34. *Papuan Villager*, Vol. 3, No. 10, 15 October 1930, p. 6.
35. *Papuan Courier*, 5 March 1926.
36. Ibid., 9 April 1926.
37. Territory of Papua, *Annual Report 1925-26*, para. 472.
38. *Papuan Courier*, 2 January 1925. The two films mentioned were *Kismet*, which featured a love affair between a white lady and an Eastern gentleman, and *Peacock Alley*.
39. *The Bulletin*, 8 April 1926.
40. *Papuan Courier*, 15 September 1925.
41. Herbert to Minister for Home and Territories, 25 December 1920, CAO:CRS G76, Item 22.
42. This apt metaphor is S. W. Reed's. He was writing about Australians in the Mandated Territory in *The Making of Modern New Guinea*, Philadelphia, 1943, p. 128. The lid in Port Moresby was very much thinner.
43. *Papuan Courier*, 23 April 1926.
44. Ibid., 20 November 1925.
45. Ibid., 9 October 1925.
46. Territory of Papua, *Annual Report 1925-26*, paras. 110-13.
47. *The Crocodile*, p. 24.
48. *The Bulletin*, 18 February 1926.

49. Union of South Africa, *Report of the Commission* . . . , sec. 110, pp. 24-5.
50. Testimony of Stephen Ame.
51. The whole episode has been described and analysed by Edgar Morin in *Rumour in Orleans*, London, 1971.
52. J. T. Bensted, 'Sir Hubert Murray of Papua', *South Pacific*, Vol. 7, No. 5, October 1953, p. 707.

Chapter 3

1. His Excellency to the Minister of State for Home and Territories, 10 September 1925, CAO:CRS A518, Item D840/1/5.
2. *Papuan Courier*, 30 December 1930.
3. Ibid., 28 August 1925.
4. Ibid., 18 September 1925. Two marks suggest that the petition was the work of E. A. James. The use of 'womenfolk' and 'township', both favourite *Courier* words.
5. Legislative Council, Meeting No. 6, *PD* 1925, p. 31.
6. His Excellency to Minister of State for Home and Territories, 10 September 1925, CAO:CRS A518, Item D840/1/5.
7. Ibid.
8. Before 1918, the volume has been badly damaged by insects and water and is almost illegible.
9. 10 September 1925, CAO:CRS A518, Item D840/1/5.
10. *Papuan Courier*, 25 September 1925.
11. His Excellency to Minister of State for Home and Territories, 14 March 1933, CAO:CRS A518, Item D840/1/5.
12. Central Court, Register of Criminal Cases, Vol. 7, No. 392, NA.
13. Ibid., Vol. 7, No. 376.
14. CAO:CRS A518, Item D840/1/5.
15. 29 September 1925, CAO:CRS A518, Item D840/1/5. The report was out of print and only two copies were available. Home and Territories kept one and sent the other to Port Moresby on 4 March 1926.
16. R. T. Gore, *Justice versus Sorcery*, Brisbane, 1965, p. 260.
17. His Excellency to Minister of State for Home and Territories, 12 January 1926, CAO:CRS A518, Item D840/1/5.
18. *Papuan Courier*, 8 January 1926.
19. Dr Sir Hari Singh Gour, *The Penal Code of India*, 7th ed., Vol. III, Allahabad, 1963, p. 1863.
20. His Excellency to Minister of State for Home and Territories, 12 January 1926, CAO:CRS A518, Item D840/1/5.
21. Legislative Council, Meeting No. 1, *PD* 1926, pp. 1, 2.
22. No one seems to have mentioned the case of indecently dealing with the eight year old.
23. Bensted, 'Sir Hubert Murray of Papua', p. 707.
24. Legislative Council, Meeting No. 1, *PD* 1926, pp. 6-13.
25. The Commissioners, Union of South Africa, *Report of Commission* . . . , also note the fact that while a great many witnesses believed that 'congregation of large numbers of natives in mining areas' was a danger, in fact it was not the 'mine boys' who assaulted white women (section 42, p. 14).
26. His Excellency to Minister of State for Home and Territories, 12 January 1926, CAO:CRS A518, Item D840/1/5.

Chapter 3—Cont'd

27. 'Native Women and Children', typescript of a paper by Sir Hubert Murray, 25 July 1922, sent to Mrs Anna Wicksell, Swedish representative to the League of Nations and member of the Permanent Mandates Committee, Murray Papers, NL.
28. See Chapter 1.
29. 2 November 1925, CAO:CRS G69, Item 12/38.
30. 5 May 1926, Murray Papers, NL.
31. *The Bulletin*, 4, 18, 25 February 1926.
32. There was no such regulation forbidding the employment of women, only one saying that women were not to be removed from their villages more than a certain distance. Women from local villages could have been employed in domestic service. Some were. Government House employed women as laundresses according to the recollection of Sir Hubert Murray's daughter, Mrs Mary Pinney.
33. *The Bulletin*, 8 April 1926.
34. Pers. comm., K. Inglis.
35. 9 February 1926.
36. House of Representatives, *PD* 1926, Vol. 112, 5 February, p. 746.
37. 'Alone' meant with a line of carriers and policemen.
38. *Adelaide Advertiser*, 12 January 1926. Cutting in Murray's cutting book, Murray Papers, NL.
39. *Hobart Mercury*, 13 February 1926, ibid.
40. Undated but before 17 March 1926, CAO:CRS A 432 29/4243.
41. Ibid., note on above minute, dated 26 March 1926.
42. *Papuan Courier*, 15 January 1926.
43. Gov. Sec. to A. R. M. Rigo, 13 January 1926, A/248, Item 98/A151/26, NA.
44. Testimony of Stephen Ame, Beipa'a village.
45. Ivan Champion, pers. comm. He recalls only that they were not to be engaged as house servants.
46. 7 July 1928, R. M.'s office, Cape Nelson, A328, NA.
47. *Papuan Courier*, 25 July 1930.
48. C. W. Abel Papers, Minutes of Intermission Conference, 8 March 1926.
49. *Sir Hubert Murray of Papua*, pp. 236-7.
50. Bensted, 'Sir Hubert Murray of Papua', p. 707.
51. H. W. Champion, pers. comm., 7 July 1970. H. W. Champion died in May 1972.

Chapter 4

1. Lett, *Sir Hubert Murray of Papua*, p. 237.
2. Under Section 420A of the Criminal Code which had been inserted by No. 15 of 1920.
3. *Papuan Courier*, 6 June 1930.
4. Judge Herbert to Murray, 20 September 1927, CAO:CRS A518, Item D840/1/5. Judge Herbert left Papua in 1928 to become Administrator of Norfolk Island.
5. Territory of Papua, *Annual Report, 1928-29*, p. 3.
6. 'The Pattern of Race Relations', p. 45.
7. *Papuan Courier*, 5 July 1929 and 28 June 1929.
8. Kiwais come from the Fly river mouth, Orokaivas from the Northern Division.
9. Report by the European Constable T. P. Gough, His Excellency to Prime Minister, 8 November 1929, CAO:CRS

A518, Item D840/1/5. Papuan
affairs had been removed from
the Department of Home and
Territories to the Prime
Minister's Department in 1928.

10. His Excellency to Prime Minister,
9 November 1929, CAO:CRS
A518, Item D840/1/5.

11. Report from T. P. Gough to
Government Secretary,
8 November 1929. CAO:CRS
A518, Item D840/1/5.

12. The records of the Magistrate's
Court, Central Division, held in
the Papua New Guinea National
Archives go back only to 1937.

13. *Papuan Courier*, 3 January 1930.
Report of Magistrate's Court.

14. Ibid., 27 June 1930. This fact
about Miaro's case was revealed
later as part of the report of
another case involving the
judge's wife.

15. Gore, *Justice versus Sorcery*,
pp. 91-2; also Sergeant Bagita,
'The Execution of Karo', *Kovave*,
Vol. 3, No. 1, 1971, pp. 15-19.

16. *Papuan Courier*, 10 January 1930.

17. Executive Council Minutes, No. 1
of 1930, CAO:CRS G64, Item 8.
Those present were: the
Lieutenant Governor,
Government Secretary,
Commissioner of Lands, Chief
Medical Officer, Official Secretary,
Commissioner for Native Affairs
and Treasurer.

18. Prime Minister to Murray,
12 January 1930, CAO:CRS
A518, Item A242/3/1.

19. His Excellency to Prime Minister,
5 April 1930, CAO:CRS A518,
Item D840/1/5.

20. 13 January 1930, Murray Papers,
NL.

21. Executive Council Minutes,
Meeting No. 2, 1930, CAO:CRS
G64, Item 8.

22. *Papuan Courier*, 17 January
1930.

23. Ibid.

24. Ibid.

25. Ibid., 24 January 1930, 31 January
1930.

26. CAO:CRS A518, Item F840/1/5,
Pt 1.

27. His Excellency to Prime Minister,
5 April 1930, CAO:CRS A518,
Item D840/1/5.

28. His Excellency to Prime Minister,
9 May 1930, CAO:CRS A518,
Item D840/1/5.

29. Order in Council, 7 February
1930 made under Native Labour
Ordinance. Gazetted 5 March
1930, p. 45.

30. His Excellency to Prime Minister,
8 February 1930, CAO:CRS A518,
Item D840/1/5.

31. *Papuan Courier*, 14 February
1930.

32. His Excellency to Prime Minister,
5 April 1930, CAO:CRS A518,
Item D840/1/5.

33. Stuart, *Port Moresby*, p. 180.

34. Lett, *Sir Hubert Murray of
Papua*, p. 237.

35. Paper from deputation, p. 2,
CAO:CRS A518, Item D840/1/5,
pp. 1-2.

36. *Papuan Courier*, 11 April 1930.

37. Territory of Papua, *Annual
Report 1929-30*, p. 3: *1930-31*,
p. 10.

38. Murray to Gilbert, 1 May 1931,
quoted in Lett, *Sir Hubert
Murray of Papua*, p. 247.

39. His Excellency to Prime Minister,
5 April 1930, CAO:CRS A518,
Item D840/1/5.

40. Ibid.

41. Ibid.

42. *Papuan Courier*, 25 April 1930.

43. His Excellency to Prime Minister,
9 May 1930, CAO:CRS A518,
Item D840/1/5.

Chapter 4—Cont'd

44. G64, Item 8, Meeting No. 14 of 1930, NA.
45. His Excellency to Prime Minister, 9 May 1930, CAO:CRS A518, Item D840/1/5.
46. CAO:CRS A432, Item 1930/01595.
47. *Papuan Courier*, 9 May 1930.
48. His Excellency to Prime Minister, 8 December 1920, CAO:CRS A518, Item D840/1/5.
49. Legislative Council, Meeting No. 1, *PD* 1930, p. 13.
50. Lett, *Sir Hubert Murray of Papua*, p. 237.
51. His Excellency to Prime Minister, 7 June, 28 July, 8 August 1930, CAO:CRS A518, Item D840/1/5.
52. See Gore, *Justice versus Sorcery*, pp. 91-2, and Sergeant Bagita, 'The Execution of Karo'.
53. His Excellency to Prime Minister, 8 August 1930, CAO:CRS A518, Item D840/1/5.
54. His Excellency to Prime Minister, 3 January 1931, CAO:CRS A518, Item D840/1/5.
55. His Excellency to Prime Minister, 7 April 1930, also 16 December 1932, CAO:CRS A518, Item D840/1/5.
56. *Papuan Courier*, 7 March 1930.
57. His Excellency to Prime Minister, 16 December 1932, CAO:CRS A518, Item D840/1/5.
58. Legislative Council, *PD* 1930, 17 July, pp. 5-6.
59. *Papuan Courier*, 4 April 1930.
60. Ibid., 10 April 1930.
61. CAO:CRS A432, Item 1930/01595. The number of non-Papuan females in the Port Moresby census area in 1933 was 283.
62. They were discharged, or the charges were quashed or they were remanded on their own recognisances.
63. Evidence in Central Court,

Papuan Courier, 27 June 1930.
64. 9 November 1931, CAO:CRS A518, Item D840/1/5. He was commenting on a piece in *The Bulletin*, 30 September 1931, in which the writer claimed to have heard a 'big coal black Orokolo savage' boast of the many favours he had stolen from 'the white woman'.
65. CAO:CRS A432, Item 30/1/1595.

Chapter 5

1. His Excellency to Prime Minister, 7 June 1930, CAO:CRS A518, Item D840/1/5.
2. His Excellency to Prime Minister, 16 December 1932, CAO:CRS A518, Item D840/1/5.
3. Hides, *Savages in Serge*, p. xiii.
4. Many of these activities were revealed in the case of Oelrichs, a Resident Magistrate whose own activities were the subject of an inquiry in 1914. Confidential Despatches to the Minister for External Affairs, 30 May 1910 to 10 March 1914, CAO:CRS G82, Item 2.
5. See Chapter 1.
6. *Pacific Islands Monthly*, Vol. XI, No. 10, 15 May 1941, p. 36. The correspondent was Mrs Mollie Lett.
7. *Papuan Courier*, 21 March 1930.
8. Circular Instructions, 1931, 24(iv), p. 15. The Instruction was first sent out in 1918.
9. *Papuan Villager*, Vol. 3, No. 12, 15 December 1931, p. 96.
10. J. H. P. Murray in Territory of Papua, *Annual Report 1933-34*, p. 6.
11. Champion to Prime Minister, 19 December 1933, CAO:CRS A518, Item D840/1/5.

12. Gonorrhoea takes, in the majority of cases, from two to five days to incubate (R. S. Morton, *Venereal Diseases*, Harmondsworth, 1966, p. 53).

13. 6 January 1934.

14. The charges were stated thus in a memorandum later presented to the Acting Lieutenant-Governor by A. P. Lyons, Director of Public Works, 20 January 1934, CAO:CRS A518, Item D840/1/5.

15. *Papuan Courier*, 19 January 1934.

16. Quoted by A. P. Lyons, 'Rex v [Gorumbaru], alias Stephen', 20 January 1934, p. 1, CAO:CRS A518, Item D840/1/5. The *Macdhui* was one of Burns Philp's ships on the regular run between Sydney and Port Moresby.

17. Ibid.

18. *Papuan Courier*, 19 January 1934.

19. A. P. Lyons, 'Rex v [Gorumbaru], alias Stephen', 20 January 1934, p. 3, CAO:CRS A518, Item D840/1/5.

20. Bensted, 'Sir Hubert Murray of Papua', p. 677.

21. In Re Native Stephen [Gorumbaru] Sentenced to Death, 18 January 1934, CAO:CRS A518, Item D840/1/5.

22. See R. T. Gore, 'The punishment for crime among natives', Appendix A, Territory of Papua, *Annual Report, 1929-30*, pp. 20-2.

23. See 'Raping Young Females' in R. F. Carter, *Criminal Law of Queensland*, Sydney, 1969, p. 327.

24. A. P. Lyons, 'Rex v [Gorumbaru], alias Stephen', 20 January 1934, p. 3, CAO:CRS A518, Item D840/1/5.

25. Champion to Prime Minister, 23 January 1934, CAO:CRS A518, Item D840/1/5.

26. *The Bulletin*, 31 January 1934, p. 33.

27. *Pacific Islands Monthly*, Vol. IV, No. 6, 22 January 1934, p. 6.

28. Murray to Lady Mary Murray, 11 May 1933, in West, *Letters*, p. 155.

29. Pers. comm. from Ian Stuart, Rector of St John's Anglican church, Port Moresby.

30. Murray to Patrick, 18 February 1934, in West, *Letters*, p. 164.

31. Ibid.

32. Territory of Papua, *Annual Report, 1933-34*, p. 6.

33. Minute dated 14 September 1934 from the Prime Minister's Department for the information of the Minister and attached to a copy of the ordinance. The minute recommended that the Governor General be advised not to disallow the ordinance, CAO:CRS A518, Item D840/1/5.

34. Legislative Council, *PD* 1934, 10-12 July, pp. 9-14.

Chapter 6

1. It was not the last. In 1952, six years before the ordinance was repealed, a man was hanged for attempted rape. Four other men were sentenced to death between 1934 and 1958, but these had their sentences commuted.

2. Pers. comm., 7 May 1970.

3. Pers. comm., 21 June 1970. This was always said in southern parts of the United States after a lynching. See Gunnar Myrdal, *An American Dilemma*, New York, 1962, p. 678.

4. His crime was 'stroking the arm of Mrs. B. at Port Moresby in the early morning', Register of Criminal Cases, Vol. IX, No. 396, NA.

5. The table is altogether inaccurate. R. B. Joyce, *Sir*

Chapter 6—Cont'd
William McGregor, Melbourne, 1971, p. 185, states that between 1888 and 1898 McGregor hanged eleven natives.

6. S. H. Johnson, 'Criminal Law and Punishment' in *Fashion of Law in New Guinea*, Sydney, 1969, p. 85. My italics.
7. Stuart, *Port Moresby*, p. 252.
8. See Chapter 2.
9. The book was not published until 1943, although submitted for publication in 1938, because the head of the printing firm to which it had been submitted thought it 'unclean'. It was not until the manager of the publishing department, who had recommended its publication in 1938, started his own publishing business, that the book appeared. (Preface, p. 9).
10. Murray to Patrick, 2 November 1933, West, *Letters*, pp.124-5.
11. 'Memories of British New Guinea 1908-15', typescript, MS 686, pt. 1, ML.
12. Confidential despatch to the Minister for Home and Territories, 12 December 1913, CAO:CRS G82, Item 1.

Epilogue

1. Johnson, 'Criminal Law and Punishment', p. 85.
2. Pers. comm. from Sir Donald Cleland, then Administrator.

BIBLIOGRAPHY

A. MANUSCRIPTS

Commonwealth Archives Office

Attorney-General's Department, Correspondence Files, Annual Single Number Series, CRS A432, 're capital punishment in Papua and New Guinea 1930-1', Item 1930/01595.

Commonwealth Accession (CP), No. 1:

Personal Papers of Sir J. H. P. Murray *c.* 1910-37 [Papua], set 26.

Notebooks of Sir J. H. P. Murray as Judge of the Central Court, 1905-40, [Papua], set 27.

Personal Papers of H. L. Murray as Official Secretary and as Administrator, 1916-41 [Papua], set 29.

Commonwealth Accession (CP), No. 802:

Classified prints of photographs relating to Papua and New Guinea, 1904-54 [Department of Territories, Central Office], set 1.

Commonwealth Record Series (CRS), Correspondence Files, Multi-number System Classes relating to External Territories, 1928-56, A518.

Correspondence Files, Annual Single Number System, 1903-38, CRS A1. In this series, certain papers in File 25/18522 'Deportation of Undesirables, Papua 1907-26' are closed to access.

Mitchell Library, Sydney

Evan R. Gill, collections of photos, articles, pamphlets, journals on Papua, 1924-38.

——, Press Cuttings on Papua, 1920-59, Parts 1, 2, 3.

Lewis Lett, Papua its People and its Promise, A3020.

Sir Hubert Murray Papers, A3138-42.

J. E. Nixonwestwood, Memories of British New Guinea (Papua) . . . 1908-15. ML 686.

O. C. Stone, 'Descriptions of Port Moresby and Neighbourhood, New Guinea', Paper read before Royal Geographical Society, 8 May 1876.

National Archives of Papua New Guinea

Correspondence Files, 1921-42 [Lieutenant-Governor Official Secretary, Papua], CRS G69.

Minute Books, 1888-1942 [Executive Council, B.N.G. and Papua], CRS G64.

Resident Magistrate's Office, Cape Nelson: Circulars received from the Commissioner for Native Affairs, 1914-32, A328.

Register of Criminal Cases Central Court, Papua, A700.

Rigo Correspondence Files 1920-40 [Assistant Magistrate's Office], File 7, A248.

Special Bundles: files of correspondence, station journals, patrol reports from out-stations, 1890-1941 [Government Secretary, B.N.G. and Papua], CRS G91.

Volumes of Confidential Despatches to Minister for External Affairs and Minister for Home and Territories, 1908-21 [Lieutenant-Governor, Papua], CRS G82.

Volumes of Despatches from Department of External Affairs and Department of Home and Territories, 1908-21 [Lieutenant-Governor, Papua], CRS G71.

Volumes of Papuan Despatches sent, 1908-21 [Lieutenant-Governor, Papua], CRS G76.

National Library of Australia

Atlee Hunt Papers, MS. 52.
J. T. Bensted Papers, MS. 2057.
Lewis Lett Papers, MS. 2039.
London Missionary Society Letters (microfilm), G309.
Murray Family Papers, MS. 565.

Registrar General's Office, Port Moresby

Papuan Marriages, 1892-1941, 4 vols.

University of Papua New Guinea, Port Moresby

C. W. Abel Papers, New Guinea Collection.

B. PUBLISHED OFFICIAL MATERIAL

Commonwealth of Australia

Acts of the Commonwealth of Australia, Vol. IV, 1905.

British New Guinea, *Report of Commission of Enquiry into the Present Conditions including the Method of Government of the Territory of Papua, and the Best Means for their Improvement. Together with Minutes of Evidence, Appendices and Map*, Melbourne, 1907.

Census of the Commonwealth of Australia, taken for the night between 3rd and 4th April 1921, 2 vols., Melbourne, 1925.

Census of the Commonwealth of Australia for 30th June 1933, 3 vols., Canberra, 1937-40.

Commonwealth Gazette, 1921, 1925.
Parliamentary Debates, Vol. XV, 1903.
Parliamentary Papers, 1914-19.
Votes and Proceedings, 1926.
Year Book, No. 26, 1932.

Territory of New Guinea

Laws of the Territory of New Guinea, Vol. XIII, Canberra, 1934, 1935 and 1936.

Territory of Papua

Annual Reports, 1902-
Anthropological Reports, Nos. 1-16, 1922(?)-1936.

Circular Instructions, 1931.

Government Gazette, 1908-

Information for the Guidance of Newly Joined Patrol Officers, 1920.

Laws passed in the Territory of Papua, 1920-34. Annual volumes published with Tables, Appendixes, Index and Statutory Rules.

Legislative Council Debates, 1909-40, 1958.

Union of South Africa

Report of the Commission appointed to enquire into Assaults on Women, Cape Town, 1913. Printed in Union of South Africa, *Printed Annexures to the Votes and Proceedings of the House of Assembly*, 3rd session, 1st Parliament, Vol. VII, 1913.

C. NEWSPAPERS AND PERIODICALS

The Bulletin, Sydney, 1925, 1926, 1930, 1933, 1934

Pacific Islands Monthly, first publication 1932 to 1946

Papuan Courier, 1920-

Papuan Villager, 1929-39

Rabaul Times, 1926-37

Sydney Morning Herald

D. BOOKS, ARTICLES, THESES, etc.

Abel, R. W., *Charles W. Abel of Kwato*, New York, 1934.

Allen, Percy S. (ed.), *Stewart's Handbook of the Pacific Islands*, Sydney, 1923.

Armstrong, W. E., *Report on Native Taxation*, Anthropology Report, No. 2, Port Moresby, 1922.

Australian Encyclopaedia, Sydney, 1962.

Bagita, Sergeant, 'The Execution of Karo', *Kovave*, Vol. 3, No. 1, 1971.

Belshaw, C. S., *The Great Village*, London, 1957.

Bensted, J. T., 'Sir Hubert Murray of Papua', *South Pacific*, Vol. 7, Nos. 4-5, 1953.

Biskup, Peter, 'Foreign Coloured Labour in German New Guinea,' *Journal of Pacific History*, Vol. 5, 1970.

Bodger, John D., *Fuzzy Wuzzy Angels*, Sydney, 1944.

Bolt, Christine, *Victorian Attitudes to Race*, London, 1971.

Bridges, Philippa, 'Afoot in Papua, 1923', *Proceedings of the Royal Geographical Society of Australasia, South Australian Branch*, Vol. 25, 1925.

—— , *A Walkabout in Australia*, London, 1925.

Brown, B. J. (ed.), *Fashion of Law in New Guinea*, Sydney, 1969.

Carter, R. F., *Criminal Law of Queensland*, 3rd ed., Sydney, 1969.

Chalmers, James and Gill, W. Wyatt, *Work and Adventure in New Guinea 1877 to 1885*, London, 1885.

Cheeseman, Evelyn, *The Two Roads of Papua*, London, 1935.

Chignell, A. K., *An Outpost in Papua*, London, 1911.

Country Women's Association, *A Guide to Newcomers to Papua New Guinea*, Port Moresby, n.d.

Eri, Vincent, *The Crocodile*, Brisbane, 1970.

Feetham, J. O., *From Samarai to Ambasi*, Sydney, 1917. (In the Gill pamphlet collection, Mitchell Library, Sydney.)

Gore, R. T., *Justice versus Sorcery*, Brisbane, 1965.

Griffin, H. L., *An Official in British New Guinea*, London, 1925.

Grimshaw, Beatrice, *Isles of Adventure*, London, 1930.

——, *The New New Guinea*, London, 1911.

——, *The Sands of Oro*, London, 1924.

——, *White Savage Simon*, Sydney, 1919.

Groves, M. C., 'Dancing in Poreporena', *Journal of the Anthropological Society of Great Britain and Ireland*, Vol. 84, 1954.

——, 'Hubert Murray: the Australian Pro-Consul', Review, *Journal of Pacific History*, Vol. 4, 1969.

Gour, Hari Singh, *The Penal Code of India*, 7th ed., Vol. III, Verma, S. K. and Subrahmanyan, E. E. (eds.), Allahabad, 1963.

Hall, Mary, *A Woman in the Antipodes*, London, 1914.

Holmes, J. H., *In Primitive Papua*, London, 1924.

Hides, J. G., *Savages in Serge*, London, 1938.

——, *Through Wildest Papua*, London, 1935.

Johnson, S. H., 'Criminal Law and Punishment', in Brown, B. J. (ed.), *Fashion of Law in New Guinea*, Sydney, 1969.

Joyce, R. B., *Sir William McGregor*, Melbourne, 1971.

Keelan, Alice Jeanetta, *In the Land of Dohori*, Sydney, 1929.

Lambert, S. M., *A Doctor in Paradise*, Melbourne, 1942.

Lawes, W. G., 'Notes on New Guinea and Its Inhabitants', *Journal of the Royal Geographical Society*, October 1880.

Lett, Lewis, *Sir Hubert Murray of Papua*, Sydney, 1949.

Lightfoot, Gerald (ed.), *Proceedings of the Pan-Pacific Science Congress, Australia, 1923*, Melbourne, 1924.

McLaren, Jack, *Fagola's Daughter*, Sydney, 1923.

——, *Feathers of Heaven*, Sydney, 1921.

——, *The Money Stones*, Sydney, 1933.

——, *The Oil Seekers*, Sydney, 1921.

Mason, Philip, *Patterns of Dominance*, London, 1970.

Mercer, Harold, *Amazon Island, A Romance of the Pacific*, Sydney, 1933.

Monckton, C. A. W., *Last Days in New Guinea*, London, 1922.

——, *Some Experiences of a New Guinea Resident Magistrate*, London, 1921.

Moresby, John, *Discoveries and Surveys in New Guinea and the D'Entrecasteaux Islands*, London, 1876.

Morin, Edgar, *Rumour in Orleans*, London, 1971.

Morton, R. S., *Venereal Diseases*, Harmondsworth, 1966.

Murray, J. H. P., *Anthropology and the Government of Subject Races*, Port Moresby, 1933.

——, *Indirect Rule in Papua*, Port Moresby, 1928.

——, *Native Administration in Papua 1861-1940*, Port Moresby, 1929.

——, 'Offences by Natives', Paper No. 32, Vol. II, *Commonwealth Parliamentary Papers*, Session 1914-17.

——, *Papua of Today*, London, 1925.

161

——, *Papua or British New Guinea*, London, 1912.

——, 'Report of H. E. the Lieutenant-Governor of Papua to the Honourable the Minister for Home and Territories on an article on "Three Power Rule in New Guinea" by Mr Rinzo Gond,' *Commonwealth Parliamentary Papers*, 1917-18-19.

——, *The Response of the Natives of Papua to Western Civilization*, Port Moresby, 1928.

——, *Review of the Australian Administration in Papua from 1907-1920*, Port Moresby, 1920.

Myrdal, Gunnar, *An American Dilemma*, 2nd ed., New York, 1962.

Nelson, H. N., 'Brown Doctors: White Prejudice', *New Guinea*, Vol. 5, No. 2, June-July 1970.

Pitt-Rivers, G. H. L. F., *The Clash of Culture and the Contact of Races*, London, 1927.

Planters' Association of Papua, *Conditions in Papua*, Sydney, 1921.

Ralston, Caroline, 'The Pattern of Race Relations in Nineteenth Century Port Towns', *Journal of Pacific History*, Vol. 6, 1971.

Reed, S. W., *The Making of Modern New Guinea*, Philadelphia, 1943.

Rivers, W. H. R., *Essays in the Depopulation of Melanesia*, Cambridge, 1922.

Robson, R. W. (ed.), *Pacific Islands Yearbook*, Sydney, 1932.

Roe, Margriet, 'A History of South-east Papua to 1930', unpublished Ph.D. thesis, Australian National University, 1961.

Seligman, C. G., *The Melanesians of British New Guinea*, Cambridge, 1910.

Silas, Ellis, *A Primitive Arcadia: Being the Impressions of An Artist in Papua*, London, 1926.

Smith, M. C. Staniforth, *British New Guinea*, Melbourne, 1903.

Steamships Trading Company, *Annual Reports*, 1933-

Stone, O. C., *A Few Months in New Guinea*, London, 1880.

Stuart, Ian, *Port Moresby Yesterday and Today*, Sydney, 1970.

Turnbull, G. M., *Paradise Plumes*, Sydney, 1934.

——, *Portrait of a Savage*, Sydney, 1943.

Turner, Edith (Mrs Lister), *Among Papuan Women*, Westminster, 1920.

West, F. J., 'Captain Barton of Papua', *South Pacific*, Vol. 7, No. 10, 1954.

——, *Hubert Murray. The Australian Pro-Consul*, Melbourne, 1968.

——, *Selected Letters of Hubert Murray*, Melbourne, 1970.

Williams, F. E., *The Blending of Cultures: an Essay in the Aims of Native Education*, Port Moresby, 1935.

INDEX

Abel, Cecil, 92
Abel, C. W., 92, 93
Aikora, 16
Armed Native Constabulary: abuses by, 120, 156n.; display by, 37; Murray on, 120; James on, 120; power of, 23, 119, 120; qualifications of, 121; search rights of, 112; Town Guard, 51, 110, 122; wages of, 55, 122
Australia: Aborigines, 4; government and hanging, 97-8; parliament debates Papua Act, 1; reaction to Ordinance, 81-2; Royal Commission 1906, 1-2; support for Murray, 43

Badili: gaol, 95-8 *passim*, 123, 127, 131; residential area, 34, 48
Bagita, Sergeant, 114, 150n.
Baniara, 121
Bannon, R. L., 23, 24, 43
Barton, Edmund, 1
Barton, Captain F. R., 149
Beipa'a village, 7, 55, 83, 154n.
Bensted, J. T., 69, 75, 87-8, 101, 102
Bertie, R. D., 101, 105, 109, 123, 126, 131, 132
Bignold, E. B., 95, 126
Bootless Inlet, 31, 69
Bruce, W. C., 40, 44
Buka Island, 124
Buna, 122
Bunting, A. H., 69, 76
Burns Philp and Co. Ltd, 44, 105

Cairns, 35, 36
Cape Town, 68
Census: Commonwealth (1921) 25-30, (1933) 31; district of Port Moresby, 25
Central Division, 11, 20, 21, 47, 121, 149n., 155n.
Champion, H. W.: acting Administrator, 123; beautifier of town, 35; dissents from death sentence, 96; supports death sentence, 127; member of Legislative Council, 69; President of Papua Club, 38; on *Papuan Villager*, 6; provides whistles, 113; recollection of hanging, 136; on sexual offences, 114; on Ordinance, 87-8, 89
Champion, Ivan, 23, 24, 136, 154n.
Chatterton, Percy, 131, 151n.

Cheeseman, Evelyn, 14
Chinese, 27, 28, 31
Clark, J. B., 70, 115, 150n.
Clay, J. R., 62, 105
Criminal Code: Queensland code adopted in Papua, 72-3, 86; amendment 1920, 53-4; sexual offences under, 82-3, 90; superseded by Ordinance, 133-4
cricket: black versus white, 56; example of Papuan self-conciousness, 92-3; Hanuabadan team, 56; town teams, 37, 38
curfew, in Port Moresby, 49, 50

Daru, 110, 128
Darwin, compared with Port Moresby, 25-31 *passim*
Dauncey, H. M., 70, 76, 77, 85
death sentence, under Ordinance, 96, 97, 98, 127, 130, 157n.
De Boismenu, Bishop, 18, 19
Delta Division, 12, 103
Dopima village, 12
Douglas, John, 34

Eastern Division, 111, 139
Ela, 32; beach, 34, 110
economic conditions, in Papua: depression, 31, 91-2; effect of Navigation Act, 44
Elevala, *see* Hanuabada
Erua, Igo, 131, 136
Executive Council of Papua: attacked by *Courier*, 100; dissent within, 96-7; meets residents, 109; non-official member on, 127; orders defence of Stephen, 126; orders whistles, 112-13; regulates Gulf men, 104; rescinds death sentence, 98; votes for death sentence, 127

films, censorship of, 51, 52; dangers of, 53, 152n.
Fitch, Captain A. S., 41-3, 44, 60, 62, 105
Fly River, 110
Fife Bay, 111, 140

Gaile, 25
gambling, 7
Garran, R. R., 82
George V of England, 41
Goldie, Andrew, 34
Goodyear, R. A., 105, 149n.

Gore, R. T.: notebooks, 59; official draftsman, 69; President of Papua Club, 38; reminiscences, 137; sentence of Miaro, 96; tries Stephen's case, 125-7; visits Samarai, 132
Gough, T. P., 132
Granville, 32
Guise, R. E., 17
Gulf Division, 12, 54, 68, 95, 100, 103, 104
Grimshaw, Beatrice, 13, 14

Hall, Mary, 14
hanging: of Stephen omitted from history, 137; under Ordinance, 131-2, 136, 137, 157n.
Hanuabada (Great Village): beauty of women, 10; cricket club, 56; electric light in, 54; meeting place, 46; population, 47; racing canoes, 37; school children, 132; skilled workers from, 5; villagers criticised, 11
Herbert, C. E.: acting Administrator, 42-4; on Criminal Code amendment, 53-4; court note books of, 59; judgments in sexual offences, 67, 82; member of Legislative Council, 69; votes against sections of Ordinance, 74-5; moves amendments to Ordinance, 77
Hilder, L. H., 101, 102
Hisiu, 117
Hula, 48, 96
Hunt, Atlee, 29
Hunter, George, 16
Hunter, J. J., 40, 43
Hunter, Robert, 16, 17
Huntley, E. S., 69
Hutchin, A. W., 68

James, E. A.: fears Armed Native Constabulary, 101, 120; article in Smith's Weekly, 124-5; attacks government policy, 98-9, 100, 104, 108; on committee to protect white women, 105; excluded from deputation, 106; on execution of Stephen, 132; member of Chamber of Commerce and Residents' Association, 62; on sexual offences in Port Moresby, 60, 94-5; special constable, 43; supports Ordinance, 69; on repeal of Ordinance, 145
Jewell, Arthur: ability, 151n.; argues for public flogging, 76; member of Executive Council, 127; member of Legislative Council, 69; moves adjournment to Ordinance debate, 74; moves amendment to Ordin-

ance (1926) 75, 78, (1934) 134-5; President of Papua Club, 38; questions expenditure, 70
Jews, 57
Jiear, Army Henry, 15

Karo, 95, 96, 137
Kendrick, R. W. T., 69
Kiwais, 92
Koita (Koitapu) , 7, 9
Koitakinumu, 22, 38
Koke, 34, 77, 108, 147
Kokoda, 96, 98, 122, 128
Konedobu, 122
Kore, 95
Kwato, 4, 85, 92, 93

Lakekamu River, 95
Laloki, 40
Lawes, W. G., 10
Laws, R. A., 52, 62
Legislative Council of Papua: amends Ordinance, 133-5; attacked by residents, 134; debates, 70, (on Ordinance) 73-8; members, 69; powers, 39-40, 57; resolves on death penalty, 115
Lett, Lewis: member of committee for protection of white women, 105, 109; criticism of book, 87; on deputation to Murray, 106; on Hula canoes at Ela beach, 48; account of Ordinance, 85-8, 113
Lett, Mollie, 137
Logan, Leonard, 113, 121
Lolorua, 115
London Missionary Society: Central Division, 4; mission house, 34; on Motu dancing, 4, 149n.; training college, 2; resolution on Ordinance, 85; see also Dauncey, H. M.
Losuia, 111
Loudon, G. A., 26, 38, 60, 62, 105, 151n.
Lyons, A. P., 126-9, 130, 134, 142
Lyons, J. A., 125, 130

McDonald, J., 23, 105, 151n.
McEncroe, M., 131, 132
McLaren, Jack, 13, 14, 15
Mahony, F. P., 105
Maloney, William, 81-2
Marr, W. C., 131
marriage, between races, 17-18, 147
Massey Baker, G. H., 104, 115
Mathews, Dr, 41, 42, 43
Mekeo, 55, 83
Melbourne, 81

Miaro (pseudonym for Papuan sentenced to death under Ordinance): Australian Government reprieves, 97, 118; removed from gaol, 98; residents' anger at, 98-106 *passim*, 115; trial, 95-6
Misima, 128
Monckton, C. A. W., 23, 120
Motu: dancing, 4, 149n.; described by missionaries, 10, 11; gambling, 49; Hiri expedition, 48; houses, 7; servants, 55; village populations, 46; *see also* Hanuabada
Motu Motu, 95, 96
Munro, R. S., 105
Murray, H. L., 68, 69, 92, 127
Murray, Lieutenant-Governor J. Hubert P.: and Armed Native Constabulary, 119-20; and Australian Government, 108, 118; on Bensted, 87-8; court notebooks, 59; on depression, 91; deputation of citizens to, 108-10; judges case in central court, 89-90; Lett on, 85-6; on Miaro's case, 97-8, 100; opposition of residents to, 39-44; on Papuans, 5-17 *passim*, 53, 78, 82, 132-3; petition to, 62-4; 'pro-consul', 32, 57; on rape, 78, 117; on residents, 112, 119; residents' support of, 111, 116; Roman Catholicism, 29, 131; salary, 38-9; on servants, 65, 103-4; on sexual offences, 64-5, 78, 109, 114, 116, 117; and water supply, 35; and Ordinance, 67-82 *passim*, 147; wife and family, 26
Murray, Colonel J. K., 130
Murray, Lady Mary, 80, 97, 98
Murray, Lady Mildred, 133
Musgrave, Anthony, 2

Native (half-caste) Children Ordinance 1922, 19
Native Labour Ordinance, 21
Native Labour Regulations 1914, 48, 49
Native Offenders' Exclusion Ordinance 1930, 112
Native Regulations: 1907, 49; 1908, 49; 1922, 6, 52, 53; 1925, 50
Native Taxation Ordinance 1918, 46
Natives (Non-Indentured Service) Ordinance 1927, 84
Navigation Act, 44
Nelsson, J. G., 62, 69, 74, 115, 135
New South Wales, 75
Northern Division, 11, 16, 154n.

North Eastern Division, 11, 16, 121, 122, 140, 150n.
North Queensland, 36, 150n.
Northern Territory, 20; *see also* Darwin

O'Brien, Joe, 23
offences against females: Papuan, 72, 79, 114, 116-17, 141, 146; explanation for, 31, 64, 66, 80-1, 85-7, 114; numbers, 64-5, 74, 89-90, 93-5, 134; Papuans warned of, 82-3; petition about, 62; punishment for, 59-88 *passim*
O'Malley, J. T., 43, 96, 127, 128
Orokaiva, 92
Orokolo, 156

Paga Hill, 34, 90, 93
Paga Point, 94
Papua Act, 1, 97
Papuan Courier: opposes Murray, 40, 98-9, 100-1; on sexual offences, 60, 94-5, 98-9, 153n.; slogan, 39; social column, 36; *see also* James, E. A.
Papuan Villager: on Aborigines, 4; on Armed Native Constabulary, 120; on clothing, 6-7; on drink, 2; editorship, 3; founding, 103; on hanging of Stephen, 136; on Papuan houses, 7; payment for, 103; subscribers, 6; on Ordinance, 103; *see also* Williams, F. E.
Papuans, 1-11 *passim*; Aborigines and, 4; character, 1; 'inferiority', 4; in Port Moresby, 48-56; regulation of, 6, 19, 21, 46, 48-53, 84, 104, 112; sexual attitudes, 12; and towns, 8-9; and Ordinance, 59-88 *passim*
Pari, 117
Pearce, G. F., 81
Petoi, 68
Planters' Association, 39
Porebada, 152n.
Poreporena, *see* Hanuabada
Port Moresby: amusements, 37; census district, 25; Chamber of Commerce (1925), 61-2; Chamber of Commerce & Residents' Association (1921), 37, 44, 52, 60; Citizens' Committee (1920), 40-3; curfew, 49, 50; description, 34-6; masculinity, 26-7, 31; meeting place, 46; Motu villages near, 46-7; population, 26, 30, 47, 151n.; occupations, 29-30, 31; races, 27; religions, 28-9; regulation of

165